TITI KUSHIM

NOT A PERFECT
Story

First Printing, 2021
ISBN 978-978-991-386-2

Safari Books Limited
No. 1, Shell Close,
Ori Detu-Onireke,
Oyo State, Nigeria
www.safaribooks.com.ng

Cover Design by Yemikush
KUSH MEDIA
www.kushmedia.com.ng

Not A Perfect Story is a mesmerizing chronicle of a young and passionate Nigerian lady who shares some of her life experiences, interestingly, in a way that is still relevant, capable of teaching practical life lessons and can trigger interesting conversations. It paints a vivid picture of the depths, in-betweens and heights of life. This book can be likened to a delectable hot pot of spicy soup with necessary nutrients as it covers issues on culture, social life, spirituality, morality, career, family among others. The author's choice of language, humour and style uniquely blend to form a captivating and relaxing piece that keeps you glued to it regardless of your age or social background. Though, it's 'Not A Perfect Story,' It's almost impossible to pick it up and not want to read till the end.

----- **J.J Omojuwa,**
Chief Strategist at The Alpha Reach & Author of *Digital: The New Code of Wealth*

There is a zest for life, a capacity for learning and a deeply curious sensibility in the writings of Titi Kushimo. In this book, *Not A Perfect Story*, the author renders a compelling, enjoyable and gritty account of what it means to come of age in Nigeria as a woman. This book is significant for the language of the author, the period it covers and the emotional truth of the narrative. Kushimo inaugurates a substantial dive into the collective consciousness with inimitable style.

– **Tade Ipadeola,**
Author of *The Sahara Testaments*.

A feat of literary expression, a delightful sojourn into the childlike innocence of a deep mind, there is indeed something in this book for everyone. This will make a good accompaniment to a mug of coffee or when the lights are low at bedtime.

----**Bimbo Manuel,**
Nollywood Actor

With this generous offering of relatable personal experiences, Kushimo has succeeded in painting a chronicle of different life phenomena that is the lived reality of many women and girls in the global South. *Not a Perfect Story* is a reminiscence of real life experiences that is bound to stir one's imagination. This book is a relishing read, not just for its alluring use of language, but also for the thought-provoking dictums that young people navigating growth and development will find useful. This book captures the voice of a generation!

-Hannah Ajakaiye,
Chivening Alumna and Knight Fellow,
International Centre for Journalists [ICFJ].

'Not A Perfect Story' is a captivating account of the experiences of a young Nigerian, whose penchant for growth and constant self-development rings through in all the pages of the book. The author adopts a relatable story telling style to address salient societal issues.
This is a book you'll enjoy reading. The humor, simplicity of language and the vulnerability of the author make it easy to connect with.
---Mitchell Elegbe,
MD/CEO, Interswitch

The author takes us through the happiness of growing up and the troubles of exerting herself on family, friends and community. By this, she puts the days of youthful ambitions in the spotlight. It's the examination of the exploits, expectations and fantasies that define her. That Titi exhumes from memories, the events that shape her, confirms the power of the past and the value of self-reflection. It's an adaptability that shows openness to learning.
The book is the beauty of family and the stories are powerful reminders of how not to be frightened by the richness and frailties of the world. It teaches us to clutch at the things that escort us into self-fulfillment. It's the celebration of the future. It's refreshing to see through this compelling prose, how the images of the past are carefully crafted as memoirs of dreams.
— Edmund Obilo,
Bilficom Media and Systems

This is a book of delightful and startling stories, of life lessons, of insights and perspectives. It questions our humanity and asks for humanness in all that we do. It's witty and filled with anecdotes. Most significantly, it gives a glimpse into the mind of a firebrand advocate in the making
- Anike-ade Funke Treasure
Author, Journalist, Media Trainer

This book is a collection of wonderful practical stories well told in an easy going manner with sound advice to readers. It is well constructed with links to all strata of society.

----Dr. Tony Marinho,
Author & Founder of St. Gregory's Specialist USS Clinic

Titi uses poetic licence to weave a memoir of her own journey to date into a profoundly philosophical look at the connecting dots that matter in this utopia of a life! Using out-of-turn vicissitudes in her life, Titi was emboldened by positive feedback from an appreciative online community via her self-styled blog to share her consolidated experiences in a permanent readable form.
The result is this laudable first time effort written in a very lucid and infectiously anecdotal style in what looks like a budding career in easy-to-digest non-fiction!
She highlights the fact that there's a reluctant budding writer and author in all of us even if it's **not a perfect story!**
------ *Ade Araoye,*
Principal Editor - Allegna Africa Expands
[https://africaexpands.com]

For most Millennials and Gen Z, we share a common understanding that adulting is hard and nothing prepares us for the complexities of life. Like myself, many young people out there are dealing with imposter syndrome, anxiety, depression, fear of missing out and pressures to meet up to societal standards. It can be isolating living in a society where success is reduced to online recognition and living a facade of our true authentic self. The strength and vulnerability exemplified in this book is a reminder that perfection isn't a sprint but a continuous journey to becoming the best version of ourselves while positively touching lives. In this book, you'll find the most precise, powerful and practical examples to pursue your passion with purpose. I hope that every person reading this comes out feeling more dignified and empowered to redefine success on their own terms.

---Victoria Ibiwoye
Founder, One African Child

Not a perfect story manuscript was sitting in my mailbox for about two weeks without opening it. I opted to open it on a Sunday morning before setting out for church. Opening it was like a bait for me, as it got me anticipating what was on the next page. The positive vibes in this book drew me back to it immediately after service.

Titi has not only put words together in this book, she has used the right words, experience, and life's intricacies to beautifully craft her story.

You will not only find knowledge in this book, it will take you through a journey that is hilarious, intriguing, suspenseful, and engaging, touching on moral, spiritual, cultural, and other facets of life.

Not a perfect story is *unputdownable!*

----Seye Joseph,
Founder, Enterprise CEO

Growing up in an African society can be quite interesting because of the communal setting, and the strong cultural influences. This exciting biographical work offers readers, a peep into the developmental stages of a middle class educated Nigerian lady from elementary classes to the life of a job applicant. The crispy language and the vivid descriptions command attention from the first page and take readers on a journey into the influences of extended family structure, strong religious persuasions, urban street culture, and the educational system on the Nigerian personality. Titi Kushimo's strident advocacy voice rings throughout this narration in an urgent bid to draw lessons out of her personal experiences and perception of the social system. The book, is therefore, a compelling read for parents, young adults, and children on how daily encounters percolates into life- long values that shape individuals and the entire society.

Muyiwa Ojo, PhD
Head, Department of General Studies, Faculty of Business and Communication, The Polytechnic, Ibadan.

For the young, Titi Kushimo has many personal stories that inspire, including the benefits of volunteering. Perhaps, the greatest reminder that this book calls our attention to, is the truth that humanity is a connected community and we ignore this reality to one another's detriment. According to Titi, we can't afford to mind our own business and drink water in a connected world.

----Motunrayo Alaka
Development and Communication Strategist,
Executive Director/CEO, Wole Soyinka Centre for Investigative Journalism

Dedication

For my maternal grandmother, Mrs. Deborah Ejinike Akinsowon, there is no way we will ever forget your legacy.

For my dear mother, Mrs. Omolara Omolabake Oyeola, thank you for being the light of our lives. Keep resting in the bosom of our Lord.

For my dad, Mr. Okunlola Festus Oyeola. I am always an imaginary daddy's girl and I wish we got the opportunity to be best of friends. I miss the idea of you.

For Mummy A.A & Daddy J.O Awe, I love you both a lot.

For Hon. Kehinde Olatunji Ayoola, you taught so many vital life lessons that I certainly would not find on Google. Thank you for always encouraging me to work hard on my dreams and for living a life so worthy of emulation.

You all are no longer here, but your loving memory is always with us.

Acknowledgments

I want to thank God for the inspiration to write and the courage to start executing the dreams in my heart.

I thank my dear husband, Tobi Kushimo for helping me elevate the quality of my thoughts through the daily choices he makes for our home. I also thank him for being so supportive throughout the time of writing, and in fact, at all times. Thank you for tenderly watching our daughter, Moshiholaoluwa and helping me secure links to ensure a brilliant publication.

I thank Moshiholaoluwa for helping me find the strength to accomplish the things I initially thought impossible. The nights I had to throw her on my back to rock her back to sleep in between preparing for an examination in the morning or completing another chapter of this book have indeed shown me another side to life.

Thanks to my dear siblings, Tolulope, Babafemi and Oluwasanmi, for always rooting for me and allowing me share their part in my story, I love you guys.

Uncle Yemikush, thank you for a beautiful cover design at no cost and being so understanding despite the back and forth it took to make up my mind.

I sincerely thank Dr. Tony Marinho, for his immense contribution to this book. Despite his busy schedule, he spent long hours on the phone with me, helping to realign the manuscript and ensuring I don't get into trouble.

I thank Mr. Favour Adeaga for doing the initial editing of the manuscript, and Mr. Olayemi Onakunle for his professional support. I am indebted to Abdulrazaq Balogun and Boluwatife Daniels for proofreading the manuscript. Thank you so much for your brilliant contributions.

Seye Joseph!!!Thank you for being my principal consultant on this project. You moved mountains and I pray that you will never lack men.

Preface

Many of us are obsessed with perfection, and for so long in life, we have felt as if we are not enough. Each time we achieve one thing, we quickly brush it aside, looking forward to the next big thing as if success is a destination. We would talk ideas down in our heads before even attempting to share. Left to us, if it isn't perfect, it is nothing. What a life!

This can make us second guess everything we do and strip us of self-confidence, which is a critical requirement for getting ahead. We lose our voice and never feel like our opinion counts because we assume that we must know it all before taking a stand on issues. We then begin to miss out a lot from life, and the people we are trying so hard to impress will keep moving on without even noticing that we are drowning.

I began to conceive the idea of this book earlier this year, but before then, I had started a series on my social media, which I tagged #ThrowbackStories and #TheRealThrowback. It was the prose version of the popular throwback or flashback idea on social media where people post pictures of themselves from the past for the sake of reminiscence. However, when I think of throwbacks, pictures hardly come to mind. Instead, I think about the experiences, moments, good, bad, and ugly phenomena that have shaped me into who I am and becoming today. I always relieve those moments to glean from the depth of lessons or, sometimes, pleasures those stories revive.

When I started sharing, I received lots of feedback from my readers, who kept reminding me when the next edition was due. Eventually, it occurred to me that I had a material that could impact people from all walks of life. But then, impostor syndrome kicked in when I decided to put the stories into a book for easier access since my website, www.sinmirella.com, was temporarily down. A self-interrogative session quickly took place and the voices in my head held a meeting to shake off the idea of authoring from my mind, and I carried on like *whatever.*

But what do we gain from running away because we believe we are not perfect?

I once stumbled on a statement ascribed to Tara Durotoye, one of Forbes' Top 50 Most powerful women in Africa in 2020. It's paraphrased as *'no matter where you are, there is someone who is aspiring to be there, so mentor someone.'* This implies that whether we feel up to it or not, we must begin to raise leaders in our various spheres of influence, and the ripple effect can result in a better society and nation.

We must stop waiting to be perfect because the perfection we seek lies in doing our best each day and positively touching lives. Perfection must then be reconstructed. It is in our perception, how we see life; the lessons we draw from our flaws, the message we share with the world, and how we keep taking the chance to be, and do better each day.

I am sure as you read, you will find something for yourself- laughter from a hectic day or the harsh economic realities in the country, critical lessons about the opportunities that show up for us every day and how to recognize and maximize them, and how never to keep a girl waiting on a date. You should also learn how to end the mom-teenage daughter 'war,' and maybe the inspiration, like me, to stop waiting for perfection and go after your dreams because ladies and gentlemen, this is *Not A Perfect Story.*

Chapter One

There is Fire on the Mountain
...... Everyone saw them, but no one looked at them ......

I was such a naughty child; so naughty I remember my mom calling me one time to ask if I usually saw something when I slept at night. She was wondering if some spirits were pushing me to be so disobedient and troublesome. African moms! It was so easy to think I was an *ogbanje*. I would scream from 4 a.m. when my mom woke us up to prepare us for school till past 6 a.m. when she left for her office. She was a banker at Union Bank in Tinubu Square, Lagos. She left me and my older siblings, Tolu and Femi, with our dad, who dropped us off in school. The landlady of our house in Pedro, Lagos, *Alhaja*, was a tough woman, but she met her match in me. She had to admit that I was a handful for a four-or-less-year-old child.

I talked so loud and firmly, even things that shouldn't be said. One time, I made a mocking comment about how our neighbours ate *ẹba* every night because of the aroma that often came from their apartment. *'These ones don't know more than ẹba"* I carelessly remarked as we walked past the kitchenette. My mom, knowing the implication of such a statement, quickly covered my mouth and whispered something like, *'shut up.'* It must have come out more derogatory than I could explain since I was too little to recall and was only told the incident years later.

I remained completely troublesome for most of my childhood. When we moved to John Olugbo Street, Ikeja, Lagos, mom enrolled my siblings and I in Morolu Nursery and Primary School, not too far from the house, say a ten-minute walk. Morolu was a choice school for many middle-income earners, and the educational standards were very good at the time. Ghanaians taught me in Primaries Two and Three. Uncle Yeboah taught my Primary Three class. He was an absolutely brilliant guy. His grammar impeccable and his afro had the same shape throughout his time as our teacher. He had a grey finger-shaped comb stuck to the back zipper of his squared black bag, with which he combed his hair during break time and when school closed. Uncle Yeboah didn't laugh much and his pet peeve was the smell of bread and butter from my lunch box. He clearly would wish I changed my meal plan but we had a time table and my mom stuck to it too religiously to compromise. On the timetable, there was noodles and plantain on Saturday nights. My siblings and I would take turns to cook our portion, which was one sachet of noodles and a plantain each. It was one of my most anticipated weekend activities. We took cereal in our cereal bowls. Mine was light green. We actually cherished the bowl more than the cereal because each person had built a bond with their bowl that under no circumstances could you use the other person's. We were so coordinated I wonder if we were even kids!

Uncle Audu was my favourite. He taught me in Primary Two. I can never forget the knife-edge creases on his carton brown pants. Uncle Audu clearly loved his job to have won the hearts of so many students such that some cried when holidays were approaching. He made us laugh and flogged us when needed. I wonder where he is now. And no, he never took advantage of any of us. It was pure platonic bonding which should be the case!

Motunrayo Ogundipe was my classmate, the primmest and proper in the class. Motunrayo had everything in order. Her uniform was the exact way from morning till we closed at 4pm. She had no single stain on her collar and her socks remained sparking. I often begrudged her for being so selfish with her water because she carefully saved it in her orange twin-shaped water bottle and fastened the long rope to her locker so that you'd quickly be caught if you attempted to take some without her permission. Ah, Motunrayo would rather go back home with the two bottles full of water than share with classmates in distress. It was always a firm "No!" even before we asked. Let your tears flow as blood; it won't get her to open the bottle. But many years after, we met again at the university, and the first words I said to her as we exchanged pleasantries were *'are you still selfish with your water?'* We both burst out into laugher.

My closest pals were Shola Anozie, Franklin Ulogho and Baba Muhammed. We were friends and we had each other's back on a platonic level but our teacher thought otherwise so he changed our seats. However, we always found our way to one another during lesson period when the class was leaner and much relaxed.

One of the incidents I'll probably not forget in a hurry while in Morolu happened one Tuesday morning. At that time, my older brother, Femi, was in Primary Six, while Sanmi, my younger brother, was in Nursery Three. Three of us attended Morolu then, and we left home together. But on that day, I had started my troublesomeness as usual, and they both went ahead of me, hoping I was coming behind. We walked to school most days since it was just some streets away. I had stopped somewhere on the way to school, crying like a destitute child. Everyone passed by wondering, yet minding their business.

But one woman, God bless her, walked up to me from across the road and began to interrogate me. It would turn out that I attended the same school as her daughter, who was about my age. After listening to my rounds of incoherent complaining, she dragged me to her gate, wiped my tear-soaked face with tissue, and gave me Peanut snacks and a pencil because those were the two words she managed to pick from my grumblings. She then took me to school and handed me to the teacher. She must have said something that made me escape punishment for getting to school so late.

When the school closed, I showed my mom the stuff she gave me, and she immediately demanded I walk her to the woman's house. They both talked and perhaps shared notes on dealing with difficult kids since she had one herself, and that's why she could intervene so effortlessly. She became my foster mom from thence, always checking when she ran into us at the school. I miss days when the community actually joined hands to raise kids, when the other person's business was yours as well. Today, it's *"mind your business and drink water."* Hmm, I'm not sure if that is proving to be the best approach to doing life because people need support, whether they ask for it or not.

I understand some might simply be prying into other people's predicament to make them a laughing stock, or it just suits them to see the other person in distress. Still, the truth remains that there are good people out there, and if we say we should close our eyes for evil to pass away, we might not know when good will pass as well. Issues like domestic violence, child abuse, and rape persist today partly because we sometimes do not speak up; we simply 'mind our own business' when we see these things happen.

While social media has strengthened the campaigns against these despicable acts, when the chips are down, justice hardly prevails. In her book, *Where is your Wrapper,* Bisi Adeleye-Fayemi, the First Lady of Ekiti State, alluded to a cultural practice observed in some parts of Yorubaland where a day was set aside to name and shame offenders - people who committed *èèwọ̀* [taboos] such as pedophilia, incest, wife battery, stealing and other forms of crimes considered as *èèwọ̀* in the land. They would cluster in front of the offender's home and sing to mock the person. The offender was expected to come out and dance while they sang and, in fact, entertain them with food or light refreshment. This would be proof that the offender was sober and would not repeat such acts.

While this might have a few cons, there is no denying that it curbed the rate of vices and inordinate behaviour that persist today. We need to be our sister's keeper and step in when others are in distress or when they are perpetrating evil acts detrimental to the wellbeing of society, rather than completely 'minding our own business.' You see, that business you are minding will not mind you when society breaks down completely because everyone will be affected. Isn't that the case already? The children we left destitute and hungry while sending ours to highbrow schools, home and abroad, are now attacking society, fighting back, kidnapping, killing, and invading police stations. The structural violence led to violent conflicts during the #ENDSARS movement because it was the perfect opportunity for the deprived citizens to unleash their repressed anger and feelings of oppression and marginalization. They were angry that all these years, everyone saw them, but no one looked after them, not even the government to whom they handed the power to protect them.

Popular Nigerian-French singer, songwriter, and recording artiste Bukola Elemide known by her stage name, *Aṣa*, was right years ago when she sang,

'There is fire on the mountain.'

There is fire on the mountain

And nobody seems to be on the run

There is fire on the mountain top

And no one is a-running'

I wake up in the morning

What do I see on my TV screen?

I see the blood of an innocent child and everybody's watchin'

Now I'm looking out my window

and what do I see

I see an army of a soldier man

Marching across the street, yeah

Chapter Two
Aunty T
This life is too tough for mẹkẹmẹke

When I was a child, I wanted to be a big girl, drive a big car, and enjoy my life; a *'baby girl for life'*. Don't judge me. I loved everything fancy, and I was usually so preoccupied with how I'd raise funds to support my big girl aspiration. Somehow, I knew I had to work for the good life I wanted. This was 9-year-old me.

I was going to build a school in a highbrow area of Lagos with high fees but very sophisticated facilities and all. My older siblings, Tolu and Femi, attended that kind of school – Green Springs School, Anthony, Lagos. So, I used that as my mental template. Of course, I had not heard of, or studied Karl Marx, who believed that the history of all existing human society is the history of class struggle, yet, I was conscious of class structure and how society was stratified in a way that continued to widen the gap between the haves and the have-nots. I wanted to be in the former class.

I sat in my grand mom's liquor store one day, drafting a budget for the school project. It had items like a school bus, landed property, and staff salaries. I even had a dress code for my imaginary staff. No sloppy clothing, no tacky outfits, everything must be sharp. I arrived at a total of ₦ 2,000,000. I began to brainstorm about raising funds so I could kick off as soon as possible. After editing all the options in my head, I concluded that starting a personal savings plan was my best bet, so I created a stash of all the cash that guests dashed me when visiting. Road to two million activated! or not?

My only Lagos schooling experience before then was China Nursery and Primary School in Gbagada Phase I. I was told I cried the most part, and I have faint memories of the red and white striped spread squared collar dress that was the school uniform. I would scream all day, and when my mom was fed up with the daily crazy tantrums, she took me to a doctor who threatened me with a big injection which he promised to use on me anytime I caused trouble. I was told of how I began to behave myself afterwards.

During that period, I had grown older and was living with my grand mom in Ibadan, following my parents' tragic separation. Actually, my siblings and I had always shuffled between living in Ibadan and Lagos, depending on certain factors. Mom worked hard to give us a good life when we were younger. However, she had grown in ranks at her job at Union Bank and needed more support to raise us, which her mother graciously offered.

We'd all later move to Ibadan, and this was when my big girl aspiration took full swing. We were never really integrated into the area because we were *'Lagos kids'* who spoke English most of the time. We didn't mingle, and our friends were mostly people from outside the area - school or church. However, my grand mom ensured we learned to read and write Yoruba because she taught us from *'My Book of Bible Stories'* [Iwe itan Bibeli mi], *'Listening to the Great Teacher'* [fifetisile si oluko nla naa], and *'What does God Require of us?'* [Kinni Olorun n beere lowo wa?], all publications of Jehovah's Witnesses. These remain some of the best childhood books I ever read.

......

Aunty T, her siblings, and mom lived in the building adjacent to ours. *Iya Urhobo* and her family had previously occupied it. You see, in off *Oke-Ado* street, where my grand mom's house was located, people were called either by their place of origin or their craft. Iya Urhobo was of Urhobo origin in Delta State, Nigeria. There was *'baba onipata,'* because he manufactured and sold local underwear. We also had *Iya elero,* because she operated a pepper grinding machine that served the neighbourhood at a fee and also sold essential soup ingredients that often came to the rescue for many, who were too occupied to go to big markets, or needed urgent supply of tomatoes to make, for example, a bowl of egg sauce. There was also *'Baba feremade'* because he owned a pure water making factory where the entire neighbourhood bought their drinking water. He would give out the water for free during festive periods such as New Year's Day.

Some landlords in the area had resorted to drilling boreholes in their homes since they could not afford the trouble of fetching water from the well. Citizens have struggled with basic amenities for many years in a country that prides itself as the giant of Africa. Let's not get started on this yet.

The funniest was *'Ìyá ẹ̀dọ̀'* and *'Bàbá ẹ̀dọ̀'* because they sold goat meat parts - what we call *'assorted'* or *'orisirisi.'* *Ẹ̀dọ̀* is the Yoruba name for lungs. I couldn't get over how *Bàbá ẹ̀dọ̀* seemed to successfully manage two wives in his one-room apartment and let's not talk about the scent of goat meat that filled the air each time he passed by. *E choke!* But *Bàbá ẹ̀dọ̀* cared for his family so much. He came to our house occasionally to help fix some plumbing stuff since he took that as a valuable side hustle. He was always cheerful and would laugh at jokes even when targeted at him.

I don't know why I pitied him a lot. Even now, I have a picture of his face flashing through my mind, and it still looks like pity, maybe because I feared his hefty second wife was too much responsibility for such a lanky, easy-going human. And he seemed so reserved I often wondered how he wooed two whole women or how he had the energy to sexually satisfy both of them, if he did. I often drew comfort in the fact that he was *kuku* sleeping with two women so, he didn't really deserve as much pity as I was showing. Polygamy just seemed like a disaster to me. It still does. But his wives appeared happy. They found a way to live in a structured harmony, even if it was to shame neighbours who were always delighted at the downfall of others. His first wife joined their husband in the meat business while the younger had a provision store by the entrance of their *Face-Me-I-Face-You* apartment. She fought people more than she made any sale at the said store.

......

Aunty T and her family were a breath of fresh air. Finally, someone who looked exactly like what I had fantasized about. Her mom quickly got christened as *'Ìyá Tayo'* [name changed] because their first child was Tayo. I always had a crush on reserved guys. I certainly cannot stand a life of the party kind of guy. It must have been a thing from childhood. I low key liked how Tayo never said a lot but would simply wear a naughty smile and a subtle repeated wink that gave him away as a refined, good, but tricky boy. Young girls can innocently be attracted to older boys or men, and the latter must protect, and never take advantage of them.

It is disgusting when sexual predators blame their victims for 'seducing' them. There is nothing as consensual sexual activity with a child under eighteen years; that is sexual abuse and/or rape. A child might have a crush on an adult because of her/his immaturity, but that doesn't confer the right on such an adult to crush or defile them sexually. Also, parents must not shy away from these realities. Children understand this, so we must not assume they do not or that they are too young. It is a dangerous assumption. A needed digression.

Aunty T was my fave. She drove a black Sport Utility Vehicle, which she alternated with their mom's olive green Mercedes Benz. Aunty T had a group of girlfriends with whom she partied every Friday night, apart from the numerous *owambes* on Saturdays, which mostly included her mom and younger sister, aunty Funke [not real name]. Aunty Funke was the real baby of the house; fragile and over-pampered. Aunty T fought with a friend one time, and poom! she had broken a bottle. I was scared for her and the said friend. *"What sort of thing is this?"* I thought. But then, I got to know that a lot of people like her are usually a combination of 'street' and 'butter'. That day, I saw the former. They somehow settled the matter, and things went on. I usually marveled at how these people were so bougie and *razz* at the same time. All they did was have fun. I never saw them go to work or anything. Yet, they were living the life. Ọmọ, I started rethinking. I quickly figured I didn't have to do so much to be a big girl. No need to start a school and no need for all that *wahala abeg*.

My mom already knew I had such funny tendencies, so she had been a little harder on me than anyone. I had, on several occasions, questioned her love for me. So many times, I said it to her face. Oh, dear! I was a handful.

I began looking for ways to penetrate the Aunty T circle. By then, I was in Senior Secondary School, so my swag was at its budding stage, although often truncated by my mom's many clothing rules: no trousers, skimpy dresses, and no big earrings. Ha! It took me digging up her old pictures to make a case for my sister and me. Mom wore trousers a lot; jumpsuits were her thing, and boy, those dresses were super skimpy! Oleku! Forget, 60's fashion was *litty-litty*. She had no words. I'm sure she must have wondered where I came from. But then, why do moms enjoy their youth and then turn around to give us rules? *Nawa.*

They legit forbid us from doing the exact things they did and the places they went. I'd say a better approach would be to let kids understand why certain behaviour is not beneficial to their future as against setting many rules that leave them aggrieved and uncertain about their [parents] intentions. However, there is wisdom in dealing with each child based on peculiarities and not generally set standards. I fear that a lot of parents lack a healthy relationship with their kids.

Mom had a relationship with *Ìyá Tayo,* aunty T's mother. It was a kind of cordial relationship born out of simple courtesy and the fact that they seemed a lot more exposed than the other neighbours. However, mom low key didn't like their lifestyle. *Ìyá Tayo* would pass for some confirmed *sugar mummy* if care was not taken. Picture this - low cut, blonde tint, triple lob, tragus, and fully stoned *abaya* with dangling earrings and gold-plated ankle chain on both legs. That was *Ìyá Tayo.* My dream mom. Mine was always stopping me from doing the crazy things in my head.

Society has a way of defining people like *Ìyá Tayo,* especially that she was a single mom, and no one was sure if that was by choice. But then, she was such a pleasant woman, so it wasn't so hard to overlook all other 'flaws.' She took a stand on community matters and would swiftly make suggestions about how to fix certain issues. Many times, the landlord's association forgot she was not a member because her impact was so visible. She was a leader, firm, and decisive. She did not pretend to be comfortable with decisions; instead, she spoke her mind. I wanted to be so bold.

My mom had sent me to buy her *amala* from *'Moji,'* as we all called both the woman and her store. It is widely believed that the *buka* kind of *amala* is matchless. The taste, aroma, and uncourteous attitude of the attendants, always trumps the homemade or ones sold at restaurants. If one visits a *buka*, the chances are high that the attendants would be rude. *'Eran meloo'* [*How many pieces of meat?*], *kosi change o'* [I do not have change!]. The ladies would yell, even before they take your order. The insults double if you do not buy meat or any protein with your meal. It is assumed that you must be so poor. But you see, the consumers know that no amount of insults can quench the irresistible taste of this highly sought after Nigerian delicacy. So, occasionally, we all indulged. However, I was becoming more conscious of myself. The last thing I wanted was to be caught handing out a bowl to *Moji* as she tactfully pressed in the portions of *amala*, making a hollow in the middle where she'll then lavish the *gbegiri* and *ewedu*. Ehn, on the main road? *laelae*. God forbid. What if my crush passed by and saw me? What if someone drove by and noticed I was buying such a thing. It would be better to be caught strolling out of Mr. Biggs or Tantalizers, not Moji. So, I quickly declined. Call it a terrible colonization of the mind, well, as long as my reputation remained intact.

I did not understand that local delicacies did not pale in comparison to fast, sometimes genetically modified food that was sold in the eateries where I preferred. As a matter of fact, these local delicacies now enjoy international appeal. When I was an undergraduate, Americans studying at the Faculty of Arts took delight in having *amala, gbegiri* and *ewedu* as lunch. One of them spoke of the meal in such glowing terms that I thought she was referring to her lover. I was shocked when my cousin, Olawumi, struck a conversation with me about *'fufu'*. I could have sworn she hadn't heard of or eaten it before since she was born and has lived all her life in the United States. But I was here in Nigeria, acting like *amala* was trash or some type of inferior meal. Poor colonised teenager.

Well, I made an excuse to my mom that day and somehow got away. Not long after, Aunty T called me. Hitherto, our relationship wasn't beyond casual exchange of pleasantries - *'Good afternoon Ma'*, and she'd reply,

'Aah Titi, how far?' Nothing more. It surprised me when she suddenly called me that day to help her get amala`from Moji. This was the golden opportunity I'd been waiting for. I wanted so badly to be around her. In a blink of an eye, I was at Moji, neglecting all the excuses that prevented me from helping my mom with the same errand.

I delivered the amala` and stayed back for an interactive session with Aunty T and her friends. It was my first time being in their apartment, and that was so thrilling. I casually strolled back home after believing I'd finally cemented my relationship with *Ìya` Tayo's* family, particularly aunty T. I got home to the beating of my life. My mom never hit us, except for occasional slaps on the back, which weren't strong enough to bring a tear down your cheek. So, it was an absolute shock how she beat me that day after I had foolishly narrated that I was actually sent to Moji. Another thing is that we didn't tell lies. Our faces would give us away even if we attempted. We had a bible verse against every atrocity we were planning to commit. Our relationship with our mom and grand mom was quite so important to us; we didn't want to let them down. That must have made us very well behaved, but I think we overdid it because I often struggle to get back at people who try to take me for a ride. Meanwhile, this life is too tough for *mẹkẹmẹkẹ,* and I'm particularly learning that you have to put yourself first because that's what the world would do. That means standing up for your right and ensuring you are not shoved aside, or not accepting all responsibilities thrown at you because you are considered a nice person. You might be left with a feeling of emptiness if you do not show compassion to yourself.

Anyway, apart from feeling the physical pain from the twelve solid strokes of the cane that my mother arranged all over my body that day, I was also emotionally broken because I could see pain and frustration through her eyeballs as she flogged me.

It was not about the errand; she was unknotting every bolt in my head that wanted me to be like Aunty T because she knew much more than I thought I did.

Chapter Three
D.N
I began to learn never to expect too much from anyone, no matter who they are.

One of the biggest influences in my life is my late maternal grandmother. I cannot bring myself to the idea that she is actually late because that woman was a force. I'm glad I got the opportunity to experience her and everything attached - my mom, Uncle Kayode, and Aunty Asake, her children. Uncle Kayode is the most sanguine in the family, outspoken, completely sound and intelligent. I'd always said if I ever found myself on MTN's Who *wants to be a Millionaire,* he would be my phone-a-friend option.

As he's fondly called, Sir kay has the dates of every event in his head; he reads wide, and I wonder if he would have been in politics were he not fully committed to his Jehovah's Witness doctrines. It was from Sir Kay I first heard *Taliban.* He had referred to it while contributing to conversations about Nigeria's Boko Haram insurgency. When I innocently expressed that I didn't know about the Taliban, he gave me a fusion of a surprised and disappointed look. I was about to resume 100 level as a student of Political Science in Nigeria's premier university. Good grades are important but what really stands anyone out is their level of information about relevant issues in society and how they are able to deploy such knowledge to make an impact in their spheres of influence. It is an important lesson I have learnt

Well, I took the criticism from Sir kay straight to google. Then, I found that the Taliban was a political and religious faction that emerged in Afghanistan after the collapse of Soviet troupes. Their notorious regime led to a breakdown of order in Afghanistan in the mid 1990's. The prominent girl child education activist, Malala Yousafzai was a victim of the Taliban extremist activities when she was shot on the bus on her way from school in October, 2012. She survived and has remained a strong advocate for girl child education. It is completely worrisome that the extremist Islamist group recently returned to power in Afghanistan and has taken total control. With the series of events that marked their earlier reign, there are clear reasons for observers to be worried. After promising to run an inclusive government, the Taliban have appointed new leaders in Afghanistan and the leadership composition is made up of only their members and there are no women.

Sir Kay is also partly responsible for our smooth command of Yoruba because when we were much younger, he had mandated us never to speak English whenever we were on holidays in his house with our cousins, his kids. Well, we pulled through as tough as it was.

Aunty Asake is the Cinderella of the family, even in her 60s. She is as cute as a one in her 40s, an absolutely gorgeous woman. My mom said everyone called her '*oyinbo.*' Aunty Asake liked to dress up, and we were told no one dared beat her when they were growing up because she was so fragile and could quickly fall ill after some strokes of the cane. Mom said she suspected all the illness was made up, but what's a last child without some drama? Aunty Asake dared to open my mom's wardrobe to her friends to choose outfits for their planned party one day. My mom only found out when the borrowers came to return the outfits. My aunty remains classy, a beautiful soul with such a large heart. No wonder she manages to care for so many of us.

But baby sisters would test your patience, *ehn?* I always tried out all my sister's cute outfits since she had so much then but never let me wear them. One day, I stubbornly picked one of her favourite- a mid-length silk print wrap skirt, and she wouldn't have it. It was annual convention grand finale in our church, Foursquare Gospel Church, District Headquarters. The annual convention of the church featured teenagers' presentations. The grand finale particularly allowed teenagers across the various churches that made up the district minister in songs or any other activity they had chosen.

The activities ranged from music to drama, dance, with heaps of competitiveness wrapped in feigned spirituality. It was a spiritual activity, only to our instructors because, as far as we were concerned, it was an opportunity to hang out, play, check out who sang or danced better, up our swag game and of course, catch up with our crush from the other branches. We would do the most to impress the older church members in the audience during the teenagers' week celebrations. Still, this set of audience members were hardly ever impressed because left to them, we were a bunch of sinful souls who needed urgent redemption. They simply indulged us on account of formality, and we were conscious of that ourselves.

There were three factions - the rich kids, Pastors' kids, talented kids, and the 'masses.' You were in trouble if you didn't belong to the first three categories. The tension was crazy. We weren't rich kids or pastors' kids, but my brother, Sanmi and I were talented. He danced while I sang. So, we were always relevant in the scheme of things. Thank God! Nobody talked about these things. One would assume the church is a classless society, but it is not, and the acceptance of this reality is wisdom that helps members manage their expectations and understand that the church is full of humans and not archangels.

Well, it was the grand finale for one of the annual Teens' Festival, which was tagged *'In da Club'* after a rigorous case was made to the ministers who judged the theme carnal and *'unfoursquarian.' Which yeyé club?* They queried. But after an elite consensus among us concluded that Jesus was 'in da club' where the club is the church while the members were having a party with their saviour, we simply found a bible verse to shove it down the throats of our coordinators. Well, our salvation was *kúkú* always in doubt, either way. I was the lead singer for our choice song, *'He Still Loves Me,'* by Beyoncé Knowles and Walter Williams, performed in the classic movie *Fighting Temptations*. We had rehearsed quite well, and I was ready to smash it.

My sister's skirt seemed like the best outfit to kill the show. I had barely arrived at the junction to get a taxi when she began yelling at me to come back and pull it off, but I refused. *Today na today, you cannot comman kill my shine*. I stubbornly ignored her and went ahead. Occasional thoughts of the trouble that awaited me at home flashed through my mind as I sang but I didn't let that stop me. I delivered my verse of the song excellently. Of course, after scoring Beyoncé's moves, turns, adlibs and pitch as she rendered the song in the movie like a hundred times. The resounding applause from the gallery full of young people told me it was a beautiful performance and that was all that mattered. Eventually, my mom settled the case, and of course, my sister got all the blame. *'Aburo ẹ ni, ó ń yọ sí ẹ lọrun ni'* [*She is your baby sister and is only trying to get pampered by you*]. That's how I got away each time.

As we fondly called my grand mom, Mama' showed my siblings and me most of the deepest issues of life that guide us today. Mama'was highly disciplined, classy, reliable, and stylish. She was industrious and always had an avenue to multiply wealth.

D.N was her initials; Deborah, Nike, Ejinike because she was a twin, but the news had it that her twin sister passed a few days or months after birth.

Mama'taught us to read in Yoruba; she would encourage us to raise our hands and read selected Bible verses during the book study sessions of the Jehovah's Witnesses, which were held in our home every Wednesday. She would sometimes attach rewards for whoever read well. It became a competition among little children in the *Oke Ado* congregation.

One of the major activities of the Jehovah Witnesses was the annual conventions tagged Special, Circuit and District Conventions, which were held thrice in the year, respectively. Everyone looked forward to it so much it seemed like the compensation for the non-celebration of birthdays, Christmas and other 'pagan' festivals. Because my siblings and I spent some part of our childhood with D.N, we attended the congregation meetings, studied major spiritual literature materials, and did not observe these festivals. We were clear about our reasons for abstaining - birthdays because King Herod, the only person who marked his birthday according to the Bible, ordered the beheading of John the Baptist at the request of his stepdaughter, Salome and her mother, Herodias.

There was no record of Christmas, New year, naming ceremonies or Father and Mother's Day celebrations in the Bible. The only event that Jesus Christ commanded Christians to observe was the memorial of his death. '*On the night of his passing, Jesus took bread, gave thanks, broke it and said...do this in remembrance of me...*" [1 Corinthians 11:23-26]. The memorial service is a big deal for Jehovah's Witnesses, and I might continue to attend annually in honour of my grandmother. She would have loved us all to participate even though we had moved on from practicing the Jehovah's Witnesses' faith.

Apart from the memorial, conventions were usually the second big deal. People made new clothes, large feasts of different delicacies, and so many old and new connections to look forward to. It was such a joy, especially the District Convention, which held from Friday to Sunday. We all looked forward to Sundays because it was the day for the drama session. The actors played out selected Bible stories around the theme of the convention. Really, that remains one of the best live demonstrations I've seen. So perfect. No mistakes, no errors. The actors rehearsed the whole year before the demonstration, I'm sure because, ahn ahn!! I can't remember how the cast was chosen, but I know it was such keenly contested roles that were only open to few individuals based on strict requirements. We all felt proud one time when a member of our congregation, Kayode Ikotun, made it to the cast, playing Joseph in one of the editions. The costume was perfect, flaunting his round thick, slightly bow legs. We clapped at the end of every scene, but this was louder when it featured someone you knew or a really hilarious character. The '*Àwòkékòó* [drama presentation], was often the major highlight of the District Conventions. I could pay to watch it even now.

'*Akú ayọ̀ ìpàdé oo'* [happy celebrations], members would greet one another with big hugs, smiles, and exchange of meals. Sharing was common at these meetings but not without subtle competition about who wore the best outfits, especially among young ladies and married women. The men hardly cared. They'd repeat clothes throughout the event if possible but the women had a whole collection specially designed for the convention, with the best reserved for Sunday. Well, it was all love, you could tell.

Fatumo, the convention ground, used to seem like such a long drive, but I'd later find out that *ifatumo* is actually a small village in Oyo State. Left to us, it was a journey that took forever, and we couldn't wait for that billboard that said, *'Welcome to the Convention of Jehovah's witnesses [Ẹ́kaabọ̀ sí ìpàdé àwa ẹlẹ́riì Jehovah].*

My brother and I looked forward to conventions with such excitement because it was a beautiful adventure for us. We would zealously get up in the middle of the night to start preparing but Màmá would drive us back to bed that it was too early. On some occasions, we would go with the hired bus for the congregation, which took some people who either didn't own a car or just preferred to enjoy the company of other members.

The bus would pick members up at a designated venue early in the morning and drop them off at the same venue. Grandma had a different arrangement since she no longer used a driver, so we drove in her friend's car – herself, Sanmi, my younger brother, and I. Her friend's son lived two houses away from ours. But this time, we went on the general bus. The thing with that is you could get left behind if you arrived at the pickup point a minute late. It didn't matter if they saw you crossing the road to meet up with them. As far as they were concerned, you didn't keep to the agreed time, so the bus shouldn't be stopped for you.

One time, Mama and Papa Oduntan, one of the oldest couples in the congregation, fell victim to this rather harsh practice. The couple arrived at the venue just as the bus was taking off. Well, they observed the convention in their room that day because the bus simply did not wait. I was so pained. Yes, rules must be obeyed, but there must be room for mercy. I wouldn't even call that mercy; it's the moral thing to wait for the older ones if they were running late, especially if it wasn't their usual practice. Who even says they couldn't have made an arrangement for the driver to pick these septuagenarians first in their home before driving to the general pick-up point? I had all these alternatives in my head. I only wonder why the elders and influential individuals in the congregation did not explore that.

I begrudged the bus arrangement for so long, but the thing with Jehovah's Witnesses is that there is always that leveler and the structure hardly permits superiority based on age, wealth, or status. It's the same stringent rules applied to everyone. This assertion is from my observation from practicing the faith as a child.

Anyway, the convention ground was about fifteen minutes away from the billboard.

Our faces and voices would light up. The singing in the bus would increase in volumes we never thought attainable. We sang and rejoiced:
'Then they will know, you only are Jehovah
Then they will know, your ways are just and true
Then they will now throughout the whole creation
All you have purposed you will surely do.'
A committee of lead vocals will quickly chant, *'then they will,'* as an adlib, while others took the chorus right again.
My all-time favourite was:
Can you see with your mind's eye people dwelling together?
sorrow has passed, peace at last
Life without end at last
chorus: Sing out with joy of heart
You too can have a part
Live for the day when you see
Life without end at last.

We had gone with the general bus on this particular edition and somehow arrived in Ibadan after dark. Unfortunately, that was not the practice because the convention programs usually ended, latest by 4 pm, so participants could make their long trips back to their various destinations. On this day, it had rained so heavily, and that caused massive traffic.

It was still drizzling when we got to the drop-off venue. In no time, everyone had dispersed, and the bus driver was heading his way as well. My grandma, my brother and I quickly crossed to the other side of the road, searching for a commercial cab. Luckily, we found an empty taxi, and we were soon riding in the home direction when another taxi suddenly pulled over across the road, blocking ours. The two drivers began speaking a certain language we didn't understand. Right there, grandma flung the car door open, pushed us both out, grabbed her handbag and leapt out of the car. It's not like Sanmi and I didn't expect her to act when we noticed something was off about the way both drivers were communicating, we just didn't expect it to be so fast, well thought out, and perfectly calculated.

In no time, we were half-walking, half-running through the narrow path that led to the closest landmark to our house. Ah, I felt so bad I wished there was something I could do. It hurt me so much that she had to go through all that trouble. I wished someone had prevailed upon the bus driver to help us get home because it was late and there was rain, but they all went their separate ways. That night broke me. I began to learn never to expect too much from anyone, no matter who they are. You might think they can see you need support, but they just might be too caught up with their own lives to notice.

Mama would have found a way to help others out. She would call a cab, mandate her driver to help, or do something. I'm always so blessed to have grown up in a lineage of humans with such generous hearts. They could give up their eyeballs if the other person needed them more. However, I get angry at the same time that this act of altruism is hardly ever reciprocated, and one has to always look out for oneself first. It reminds me of one of my sister's friends, who fed solely on my sister's allowance in school but locked her food safe in a cupboard so my sister could have no access. Let's not talk about the fact that she fed off my sister for the whole year on top of free accommodation, to which she contributed zero Naira and zero kobo. She later spent some time in our house where she did nothing but cross her legs, waiting for food to be served while hiding her phone charger from everyone when there was clearly a need for her to share. Who does that? People are selfish, but I digress.

We got home that night completely exhausted, but that didn't stop us from showing up the following morning. No one asked how we made it home. All smiles, no grudges, nothing. D.N is the most amazing human I have met. She daily showed us how to be human to ourselves and others. How to be coordinated, how to plan, how to give. Oh, she gave, and we are blessed for it. I don't think I will ever recover from her death, May 18, 2007.

Chapter Four
A life that was changed
May we all come to the understanding that we seek.

I f you ask me, one of the scariest phenomena for me as a child was watching movies produced by the popular Mount Zion Faith Ministries. Oh no, I had nightmares at the thought of one of their prominent productions, *Ìdè Èsù*. The madwoman painted all black with shiny white teeth, and her burst evil laughter sent serious nerves down my spine. Years later, when we met the movie's cast at a Foursquare Gospel Church convention program, I was still petrified to move close to the lady who played *Bose* in another of their blockbusters, *Agbara Nlá*.

Prior to then, the movie was adapted into a weekly soap and we were told that the streets would be so deserted you'd hear the sound of a pin drop. Shop owners would close their stores just to watch the next episode. So, if you wanted to run out of your house to escape watching the episode, you'll definitely run into the same situation. I cannot say I really saw the entire movie but the signature tune constantly played itself in my head.

'*Agbara to ju agbara lo*' [The power that is above all powers]

I couldn't sit alone on a chair and would have to hold someone's cloth tightly if I wanted to sleep, so I'm assured I wasn't alone. I developed nyctophobia - fear of night, or being alone in the dark, which I have gradually overcome.

That didn't stop me from keeping up with the Mount Zion movies since it was the only available faith-based movie production outfit. Mom also encouraged us because of the Christian values inherent in each one, and she particularly needed it to strengthen her newly found walk in Christ. She had transitioned from being a member of the Jehovah's Witnesses into church Christianity. Technically though, since Jehovah is God, all Christians should be His witnesses then. I imagine some people coming for me for this assertion but this is not a religious banter. May we all come to the understanding that we seek.

My sister had borrowed a laptop from one of her friends, Ade, of blessed memory. Ade lived a few houses away from ours, and they both attended the same tutorials towards University Matriculation Examination. So, we used the opportunity to watch movies late into the night.

Let me take a minute to talk about my sister. *Sister mi* [my sister] is the first child of my parents. While growing up, I thought she had the best of everything, and she probably did. My sister was so pampered that one time, Femi, my older brother, and I made fun of her that all she did was lay in bed and get everything she wanted. *'Omoooo,'* as my grand mom often called her, was actually everyone's fave. A lot of her male friends doubled as her admirers. *Ọmọ dáadáa* [a well-behaved child].

Sister mi bought Sanmi and I our first personal Bibles. I'll never forget. It was the New Living Translation with *a* colourful back cover. She had addressed it personally to us, stating the urgency to give our lives to Christ because 'tomorrow might be too late'. Sanmi and I chuckled over it. According to us, her *girigiri* was too much, because as far as we were concerned, we still wanted to tell a few lies here and there, and Sanmi, I'm sure, still enjoyed his occasional truancy from school with no one knowing his whereabouts despite being the class captain of his class. We feared 'giving our life to Christ' a lot because we believed that was premium bondage.

On some occasions when we claimed we had, we would sin again and start praying to God for forgiveness. One time, I promised God to take my life if I ever 'sinned' again. Thank God I'm alive to write a book. My sister autographed the Bibles, and mine read, *'1 Peter 2:2; As new born babes, desire the sincere milk of the word, that you may grow thereby.'* It took me years to understand this verse but it stuck with me, and I'll always be grateful to *sister mi* for such a thoughtful gesture.

We would snuggle around *sister mi* to watch movies late into the night on Ade's laptop. One day, she said she was playing a Mount Zion movie, and I quickly tuned off because I already had a label in my head that anything Mount Zion evoked fear. I was also becoming self-conscious and was now sure Mount Zion wasn't my brand of Christianity. I thought it was too horror and harsh. I don't serve that kind of God abeg!

This movie was 'The Covenant Child.' It was the story of an only child whose wealthy parents preferred he studied Medicine. They'd rather have a Medical Doctor as a child than a minister or, worse still, Pastor. So, they did everything possible to prevent him from becoming the latter. But as he grew, the signs were clear that he was a special child, whom God wanted to use to treat bodies but also save souls. Each time he tried to run, God found him again despite the adamancy of his parents. The scenes were getting deeper and tougher, and I did not know tears had welled up in my eyes. I had suddenly been captured without my knowledge. The storyline was doing something to me that was beyond my imagination. It got to the point that the child lost his mind, and his parents promised God that if He healed him, they would surrender totally to God's will. They wished they could save him but couldn't with all their riches. They had no choice but to let God have his way, and He did.

That night, as the parents were making a covenant with God, I was doing the same. I promised God that I'd quit sucking my fingers, a practice I'd consistently indulged in for twelve years of my life. I was twelve going on thirteen, and it had become a thing of shame for my family because they not only detested the act, it was actually becoming worrisome. *Àbí wọ́n fi ṣe ẹ́ni?* [Is this a spell?]. It is not strange for babies to suck in the early years, but this often stops before teenage at the worst-case scenario. Mine had become a lifestyle, and I mastered it so well no one could tell I sucked my fingers except my immediate family.

One time, my mom reported me to Uncle Audu, my Primary 2 teacher, and he blatantly denied on my behalf. Mom was dumbfounded. As you can tell, I didn't do it in school because I knew that would amount to reputational damage. I was the perfect child in school but a rebel at home. My mom once bought us a fable series and assigned characters to each of us. Mine was *'The two Carolines.'* Describing the same Caroline, who possessed different characters at home and in school, Caroline's mother invited her teacher to the house one day so she could see the different version of Caroline than the one she knew at school. Unfortunately, Caroline was unaware that her teacher was in their home, she refused her mom's errands and yelled back each time she was scolded. Eventually, her teacher came out and Caroline felt embarrassed. My mom likened me to Caroline and that guilt-tripped me for a long time. There was no approach they didn't adopt to discipline me. I sucked my index and middle fingers, so they soaked both in red pepper, scrubbed with bitter leaf, and bandaged with tight fabric many times. None worked.

Everyone had now left me to my nuisance behavior, but that night, I entered a covenant with God. It was real. I could sense a shift in my spirit. Hot tears flowed down my cheeks, and my siblings wondered what the issue was. *'Kílagbe Kíleju'?* [*What did we carry, what did you throw'?*] I went to bed that night as a different person. I never knew the meaning of covenant, but I figured it was something deep and binding on the parties involved. I saw how God delivered the boy from insanity after his parents surrendered, and it moved me. That night was the last time I sucked my fingers. It is not as easy as it sounds. It is as tough as a repentant drug addict. I was addicted to sucking, and it was my sleeping pill, in fact.

While I do not necessarily understand whether God has to deprive us of something precious in order to get His will done in our lives as portrayed in the storyline, I thank God for such a powerful movie. It made me realise that God can use anything to change situations. I'm not a diehard fan of Mount Zion, but there is no denying that God used one of their productions to change my life. Thank you, Pastors Mike and Gloria Bamiloye, for giving to the Lord; I'm a life that was changed.

Chapter Five
Of Single Stories
Get out of my way, idiot.

My siblings and I have always been a far departure from the realities of the environment in which we grew up. If there were any traces, something switched, and you'd never tell that we actually lived where some secondary school-age girls were popping babies. There were also occasional Street fights, especially on Sundays when there were notorious parties that usually ended in physical violence and sometimes the death of some gang members. So, it was a mix of the good, the bad, and the ugly, but we stayed classy.

We rarely had friends in the area, and my grand mom's popularity often gave us away each time we got described. '*Ooh, ọmọ Mrs. Akinsowon*' [Mrs. Akinsowon's children] or '*Àwọn ọmọ Mama Ondo* [Children of the Ondo woman]. It was probably all anyone knew about us because we gave no audience to close friendships or random visits to neighbours. We wouldn't even go out if not to school, church, or a few mandatory occasions.

Anyway, I had a friend, a classmate who was the talk of the town; the rave of the moment as at then. She had a hit single playing on Splash FM, the most popular private Radio Station in town. She had done the Yoruba version of Beyoncé Knowles' *Irreplaceable*. It was a jam. She also had '*Màbẹrù*' *[Fear Not]*, written and composed by her, blasting on the Splash FM airwaves.

Maberu, O-my baby...
Maberu O -my baby...
Maberu O-my baby ...
I will never fi e sile o
yes, O, yes oh, yes O
I will never fi e sile o...

Ajoke Adebisi loved music with her whole being; she was nicknamed after the popular American singer and songwriter Ashanti. 'Ashanti' [Ajoke] would sing at the school's end-of-year parties and talent hunt shows. She knew the lyrics to all hip-hop songs without having to buy the lyrics book. Ajoke was so consumed with hip hop music she performed at shows and sometimes nightclubs. She was indeed on the road to stardom, although many people considered her wayward because, to be honest, many respected students topping their class in all subjects more than a young girl hopping from bus to bus performing secular music interstate. However, they did not see the absolutely amazing, selfless, brave, hardworking, determined, reliable human that Ajoke Adebisi is. She suffered the danger of what Chimamanda Ngozi Adichie described in her TEDx Talk recorded in July 2009 at the Global TEDx Talk in Oxford, England, as *the danger of a Single Story*.

People often do not take the time to know others or understand why they are the way they are but quickly jump to conclusions based on popular beliefs. It's like the way they say Yoruba people from Ijebu, Ogun State, are often close-fisted. Also, that women in leadership positions are either too weak or power-drunk. This is the double-bind situation that a lot of women in leadership experience. But, till now, I do not know of any scientific experiments that have been able to verify these claims. We must avoid defining people based on general perception and give them the benefit of the doubt as long as doing so would not be life-threatening.

In any case, I was fond of Ajoke because of her entertaining demeanor. Sometimes, she did it a little too much, but you just got to love her sweet heart. You know people who overdo stuff, but you can see through their beautiful hearts and harmless intentions.

We went on to become roommates at the University. but before then, I had gone to pay her a visit in her home not quite far from ours, a twenty minutes' walk if you really take your time while doing so. Otherwise, it shouldn't take more than fifteen. We had caught up on various topics as usual and were both walking back home as she had offered to see me off since the gist was not anywhere close to coming to an end.

We got to a certain side of the tarred road leading to the major bus stop where I'd cross to the other side and have her head back home. She had made to turn when I saw this dark-skinned, almost-drunken human approach me with some broad smile. '*Hello baby girl,*' he attempted to get my attention, but I kept walking like I didn't notice while my friend kept an eye to see what was about to transpire.

Finally, he moved closer and stood in my way, so I had no choice. With a teenager's innocence and foolish courage, I looked him in the eye and yelled, '*Get out of my way, idiot.*' I'm not sure I've ever received the kind of hot slap that landed on my face faster than I could even realize. I was in shock. It was Deji [name changed], a notorious '*area boy*' everyone had come to either avoid completely or simply ignore. It was like everyone knew him except me.

I immediately realized that I was in danger because his proximity made me perceive the stench of smoke and alcohol oozing from his breath. An older woman watching from the balcony of her house began secretly signaling to me to leave immediately, or he could harm me further. She was, in fact, rolling her fingers over the top of her ear to indicate that Deji was crazy. Ajoke was dumbfounded, and we could both only communicate by exchanging surprise glances.

When I got home that day, I was so angry. First, that a stranger slapped me so hard and no one did anything; and also, because I wished someone could punish him for it. I casually ranted to my mom, and true to her completely easy-going nature, she sympathized with me and sort of moved on, but I couldn't. Later that day, I mentioned the incident to my older brother, Femi. He lost it. Even if I low-key expected him to be angry, I didn't expect it to be that mega. It was a combination of pain and anger for him.

How would someone hit his sister? How! Broda mi, as I call him, is the one who doesn't take nonsense. He always made up for the cool, calm, and collected nature of us, other siblings. He'd change it for anyone when it was necessary. He was the one who stood up to one supposed cousin of my mom, who was constituting a nuisance in our home in which we had sheltered him when he claimed that his house in Lagos was gutted by fire. We all have those lying, manipulative relatives who do nothing but waste their youthful years away, chasing vanity with their inheritance, yet expect others to pay for their slothfulness. Of course, there was no fire incident.

My mom had asked me to vacate my room so he could move in with his wife and three kids. Well, it wasn't the most palatable three years of my life. If they weren't punching each other, the man and his wife, the latter was raining curse words on my mother for not doing enough for them because apparently, we are descendants of Folorunsho Alakija.

I had barely concluded narrating the ordeal with Deji when *broda mi [my brother]* stormed out of the house. *'Let's go, let's go!'* he yelled. I quickly followed, not sure where we were going. It was on our way I found out we were heading to Deji's house. Apparently, everyone knew the house but me. By now, I was secretly praying that my brother didn't get in trouble because this Deji guy was a real thug, a proper hooligan who already had nothing to lose.

We arrived at the cream and brown one-storey building and dashed through the slightly shaky staircase leading right into the landlord's apartment. The door was open; a dark-skinned old man, clearly closer to 70 than 65, was seated, legs-crossed on the stool with a cup of something, I am not sure of, in his left hand. It would be beer or some alcoholic drink if I could hazard a guess. *'Ẹ kaalẹ sir'* [Good evening sir], *broda mi* greeted. You could sense the fear in the old man's muffled response. *'Pẹlẹ ọmọ mi, ta le beere?'* [Hello my child, who are you here to see?]. Because of the communal nature of Yorubaland, anyone you're old enough to birth is considered your child. *'Deji, Deji, la beere'* [We are here to see Deji].

The old man looked at me more closely, then at my brother, in a perturbed manner. I began to feel pity for him. He had so many questions on his face. *'Had Deji done the unthinkable to this little girl?' 'Is she okay?' 'Ọmọ mi kilosẹlẹ? Ṣekosi?'* [My child, what happened, any problem?]. Femi then explained what Deji had done to his sister and left word that he would come with the Police the next time. The old man, Deji's father, began to apologize profusely, wishing there was something else he could do.

On our way back home that day, I felt a huge sense of relief. At least, we fought back. We didn't let it slide. I wasn't sure how things would turn out initially, but I was glad Deji wasn't home because of fear of what he could have done to my brother.

A few weeks after, I ran into him. He was more in his senses than the other day. *'Hey aburo Femi'* [Femi's younger sister]. I looked over, and it was Deji. I felt a combination of fear and courage. This time, I had learnt to stay far enough and also run if need be. My guard was up, but the soft tone with which he spoke melted my heart. He began apologizing and confessing that he had been a bad boy the other day. He was sorry for what he did, and I should please forgive him. I kept walking and simply nodding along as he spoke because once bitten, twice shy. That was one of the many times he'd see me randomly and bend over backwards just to say hello.

I felt sorry for him each time because no one cared to get close to him, all writing him off as an outcast not worthy of befriending. Given his perfect command of the English language and understanding of civic issues, Deji, apparently, was a product of circumstances. He wanted to put his life in order again. I wonder if he did.

Chapter Six
In Honor of teachers
I cried like a baby for days. I lost that year again at an unquantifiable cost to my life and a financial cost to my family

Mr. Fatokun, my Government teacher in Senior Secondary School, turned out to be my second favourite subject teacher ever, after Mr. Leke Akindele, who taught me Economics while attending extra coaching sessions in preparation for the third attempt at my West Africa Senior School Certificate Examination, WASSCE.

My first attempt turned out well except that I scored an 'F9' in Mathematics, compulsory for many Higher Education courses. I had no choice but to sit for another WASSCE. This time, I had to be re-enrolled in Senior Secondary School 3 to write the examination with the graduating set. Hmm, can you imagine going back to wearing a school uniform after a befitting Valedictory Service the previous year? If anyone had told me that that would be me that year, I'd have sworn for them. My ego was punctured and self-esteem in the gutter. Some of my juniors who knew I had graduated from Secondary School looked at me disrespectfully. All of us were now in the same level *bayii*.

Sadly, despite all the trouble, the results were released and mine had a mix up which I'm yet to understand till today. Apparently, my registration number had been assigned to another candidate, or there was simply an error because I did not receive any results with my name. The one with my Registration Number appeared with the name of another candidate, so I simply had no results. I was mad. I cried like a baby for days. I lost that year again at an unquantifiable cost to my life and a financial cost to my family.

The painful thing is that there was nothing done. There was no apology and explanation, and no one brought to book for taking a year out of my life and many other candidates affected by WAEC administrative failure disease. An absolute disaster! Our family friend, who had been involved in facilitating the registration process, did his best, but I reckon the outcome was not within his control. He offered encouragement and charged me not to get weighed down because I really was. Who wouldn't? *Radarada*.

The Educational system will test your patience, and sadly, nothing ever gets done; no one is penalized for not doing their job well. Could WAEC's Exams and Records Department have followed the matter up and ensured it was resolved? What am I saying? Is it not a similar agency [Joint Admissions and Matriculations Board] that one of its staff told the world in 2018 that a mysterious snake had swallowed N36 million? I shiver from shame for such a despicable lie. This set of people only care about their pockets, and many students fall victim to their recklessness. But hey, we couldn't beat a dead horse, so we move. *No be Naija we dey?* A family friend who operated a coaching center later mentioned that there was a possibility that my result was sold to another candidate who didn't perform so well but had the 'long leg' and financial muscle to pay their way through. Wow, just wow! I wonder if these people have a conscience. I wonder if anyone has studied the emotional and economic cost and effects of such acts by unchecked WAEC staff and if such still happens today?

I then had to find a better plan for the third and, thankfully, final attempt. This time, I was angry and took the anger out on my academics. I studied so hard. I wanted that to be my final attempt, and I was under pressure since I'd declined to do a National Examination Council, NECO Examination or combine two different SSCE results.
I didn't read long hours at a stretch because of my short attention span, but I read at intervals throughout the day. I ensured to set an alarm on my table clock each time to read for an hour at once before taking a break. Instagram and WhatsApp were not popular at the time. It was just *2go*, the chat app that was already losing its popularity to BlackBerry. Facebook was not readily accessible unless a visit to a cybercafé. This minimized distractions! I often locked myself in a room after breakfast to block any chances of being asked to run errands.

Mr. Leke had an outspoken personality. He said things as he felt, and hardly bothered to keep his own secrets. However, he displayed a level of brilliance and knowledge of the subject that drew me in so much, so I had to score an 'A' in Economics in my General Certificate Examination.

Mr. Fatokun taught Government in my Secondary School. He was the only available teacher for the subject, which meant he taught all Art students in SSS 1, 2, and 3. Each class had a population strength of about eighty.

Mr. *Fatoo*, as we fondly called him, was known for flogging students by asking them to touch their toes so he could carefully arrange the strokes of a cane on the back of the student. God help you that you move before he was done; then, he'd begin all over again. If he intended to flog you twelve strokes and you got up at number ten out of pain, he'd then compel you to return to that position while he starts counting again from the beginning. I prayed never to fall prey to his canes.

One time he was to beat Bisola Famose, my friend and prettiest girl in our set. Bisola had numerous admirers, but only a few could muster the courage to approach her because of her often-sophisticated appearance and the fact that her dad was a really wealthy man before he passed, so she had that rich-babe vibe by default. She got the most advances from Senior students who began wooing her from the first day we started registration till the day they graduated. The pressure! We were close friends mostly in Junior School as I went on to Arts while she went to Commercial class. But at that time, she had become biggest deal, queen of her house on inter-house sports days, the most sought after babe in school. So, she seemed untouchable, but you see, Mr. Fatoo's canes *no dey look face*. They descended on you faster than they remembered your pretty face or your rich father. Your name on the list of noisemakers or aimless roaming about the school would easily earn you rounds of beating, and no amount of begging would save you. In fact, that fueled his anger, so we knew better than even try. He beat Bisola so much that I began to feel anger over why anyone would treat a lady in that manner. I just felt girls should not be flogged the same way boys were flogged.

It was another teacher who had flogged Aanu Babalola, the daughter of a famous monarch. The male teacher flogged her so much she brought her father to school the following day. The situation was resolved right there on the assembly ground when the king burst in on us while conducting morning assembly, demanding to see the male teacher who had beaten his daughter. Well, the principal and a group of teachers showed up, appealing to the king, Aanu's father. It was then he stopped pointing his sceptre angrily at the other students as if we were responsible for his daughter's predicament.

Anyway, my prayers against Mr. Fatoo's flogging seemed answered until one fateful day during one of the extra classes he had organised to augment the regular timetable schedule since we usually had a lot to cover. And perhaps, he simply loved his job that much. Some teachers wouldn't be so bothered unless it fetched them extra income, but Mr. Fatokun was not one of them. His extra classes held in the morning from 7 am – 8 am. Woe would betide you if your name did not appear on the attendance register. Being present in class and being able to mark the register were two different things. Let me explain. The register had two columns, one for those who came on or before 7 am and the other for those from 7:05 a.m. Yes, it was like that.

If the line was crossed before your arrival, just sit in class in anticipation of your six strokes of the cane at the end of the week. Thankfully, the classes held twice a week, so one absence was equal to six strokes and two, twelve strokes. You could only escape if you were dead and buried or in a coma. I would hurry my mom to round off her often-long prayers during the morning devotion, which was between 6 and 7 am every day. However, on the days when I had Mr. Fatoo's class, I could lose my salvation, rolling my eyes and stamping my feet on the ground if she didn't end the prayers. On many occasions, I was already on my way out when she'd finally say, 'In Jesus mighty name, we have prayed.' Well, I shared the grace at the bus stop.

I cannot remember why I was late on that very day, but the line had already been drawn before I entered. If there were a way to connive with the class captain to erase my name, I would have, so that I would cook up a lie that I was absent, but you see, that would be worse because Mr. Fatokun knew the faces of all his students so well and his ever-retentive memory would remind him that I was actually in class on the said date. Honestly, there was no way forward and none backwards either. It was me between the devil and the Mr. Fatokun's deep blue sea. I heard nothing in that class that day. All Fatoo's jokes fell on deaf ears. Oh, he was a 'humour-monger.' He cracked us up so much we quickly forgave his horrifying floggings. Science students envied us because there was hardly ever a straight face in Government class. We laughed from beginning to end.

'Oyeola Titilope,' he yelled on the due date for the whipping. He usually flogged weekly, so the pain of the cane would remind you to be punctual the following week. I was already weeping as he called the names. I couldn't make it to school the day after because I legit fell ill from the rounds of beating. My buttocks were swollen a bit, and I limped. This was Senior Secondary School 2.

There are now conversations about corporal punishment and from the look of things, it is gradually losing its effectiveness. While flogging and light physical punishment are acceptable modes of child discipline in many African societies compared to the Western countries, there are clear indications that such can come with grave consequences when abused. There have been sad cases of teachers who flogged students to death. Even a crime suspect should not be treated that way. Well, government must take a decisive stand on child abuse disguised as corporal punishment. Lagos State for instance, has banned flogging and other corporal punishment in schools.

Anyway, I never scored less than an 'A' in all Government subject examinations, and I was super upset when the General Certificate Examinations results were out, and I scored a B2 in Government.
Call him the devil or any other name, Mr. Fatokun played a huge role in stimulating my interest to later study Political Science after being rejected from the Communications and Language Arts department on the grounds that I had done mainly Social Science subjects in my University Matriculations Examinations instead of Arts.

I have been blessed by great teachers —Mr. Peter [Piro], who showed me that mathematics was not magic; Mr. Femi and Mr. Bayo Adenuga, who are the best English tutors I know; Ms. Ajani, whose Literature-in-

English classes shaped my reading culture today; Mr. Adeaga, the Agricultural Science teacher who shared his life stories with us and was never afraid to be vulnerable. Uncle Wale Ishola, who has touched so many lives with his dedication to work and commitment to helping his students reach their academic goals. Professor Emmanuel Aiyede, a father, a role model and a teacher; Dr. Irene Pogoson who showed me never to dim my light because I'm a woman; Dr. Stephen Lafenwa, whose jokes helped us relax and learn at the same time; Dr. Bukola Adesina, who is a living inspiration of how to never give up on yourself. I honor you all.

Chapter Seven
Dear Mathematics teacher
We would have judged people in the same situation but here we were, dancing off to praise and worship songs, not in honour of God, but of our dead ancestors

Mathematics wasn't one of my favourite subjects in school. I passed after three attempts in the West Africa Examination Council Exams. It was always a struggle. All my teachers would quickly spot my great writing and English Language comprehension skill and then assume I must be really smart. But with Mathematics, I was always the poorest of the poor in class, so I kept quiet for the most part. I never understood the subject despite owning all editions of *Understanding Mathematics*.

I wasn't just deficient in Mathematics; it affected any other thing that required calculations. My sister would make fun of me by asking me to add up N580 and N650 because she knew there was no way I'd know the answer. Now, we laugh over it, but it was a terrible experience. I remember in Junior Secondary School 3, we had a *Business Studies* class, and the topic was *Trial Balance*. Everyone in the class seemed to be enjoying and getting the concept except me. I didn't even understand one bit. It didn't help that the teacher was Mr. Oladejo, one of the most dreaded in the school. He beat on impulse, and if you weren't careful, you could feel sudden strokes of the cane land on your back. Wondering what you did? Nothing. He just enjoyed flexing and testing the efficiency of his new cane, which he changed from time to time. I was praying hard for the class to end.

Classmates answered questions and got rounds of applause, while others quickly chorused a loud 'yesssssss!' when he asked the almighty question, *'Do you understand?'* I couldn't respond because of fear that he might ask me to explain to the class. *God no go shame us.* I started to cry.

But now that I look back, I know many other students like me felt lost but were pretending out of pressure to belong or be recognized as brilliant.

Never let anyone put pressure on you because of the things you assume they have over you. We all have our areas of strength, and that should be our focus while we try to work on the areas where we are lacking. There is hardly any human being who possesses a mastery of all things. If you lack in some areas required to get ahead in life, you have to put in more effort to overcome the weakness to succeed. We can achieve anything we put our minds to, or at least, something close.

It was the same me in an English Language class; Mr. Ajijola had decided to conduct an impromptu debate and divided the class into two groups. That day, I spoke on behalf of my team and got the loudest ovation from both classmates and some of the teachers to whom our English teacher had bragged about me. Trust me, it was worth the hype, the most intelligent, fluent speech from a teenager. It was a debate about whether secondary school girls should be made to cut their hair or grow it in school. There was a standing rule in many secondary schools across the Southwest that mandated girls in their Junior Secondary Schools 1-3 to keep their hair low while choosing to grow it in senior school - if they so wished.

The argument was whether they should be given that choice all through secondary school. I spoke against the motion. In my opinion, girls in junior school should leave their hair low till they have the maturity to grow it and keep it neat, which only works better in senior school since many girls are forced to get their hair done on Sunday evening for school the next day. But when they get to senior school, they need not be reminded because they already have a sense of responsibility, and some even make their own hair. I also spoke that hair-making is very time-consuming, and such time could be dedicated to doing more productive things. I then cited examples of great women on low-cut like Oby Ezekwesili, who was then the Federal Minister of solid minerals and later became Nigeria's Minister of Education.

I also mentioned the legendary Onyeka Onwenu, one of Africa's most vocal female activists, a globally celebrated Nigerian singer, songwriter and actress. I had no idea that I knew all these things. Thanks to my parents, ardent readers. We watched the NTA network news at 9 pm every weekday and the epic signature tune sometimes still rings in my head. Names like Frank Nweke Jnr, who was the Minster of Youth and later Minister of Information and Communication during the second term of former President Olusegun Obasanjo; Charles Soludo, the then governor of the Central Bank of Nigeria who is now into active Politics in his hometown; Olufunke Oga, Cyril Stober and Ayinde Soaga, veteran newscasters on the NTA Network still linger. This vintage pool of broadcast experts has sadly not been reproduced hence, the mass subscription to foreign and imported TV content.

......

I had been enrolled in a tutorial for another attempt at my General Certificate Examination [GCE]. Things seemed to be picking up because I had re-read Ben Carson's *'Big Picture,' 'Think Big,'* and *'Gifted Hands,'* and felt really hopeful that I could achieve anything. Ben Carson moved from being the dullest in class to a world-renowned neurosurgeon.

Our Mathematics teacher at this tutorial, Uncle Lanre, was a graduate of Ogun State University [OSU], Nigeria. OSU was renamed Olabisi Onabanjo University after the former governor of the State, Chief Olabisi Onabanjo. He was believed to have played a huge role in the establishment of the institution. Uncle Lanre, slightly brown-skinned with his thick lenses on tiny dark frames, wore native most of the time, and he hardly played. I guess he was simply taking coaching as a viable side job. One would assume that teaching was not his first love. Well, he knew the subject so well, so why not?

One day, the class got so intense that I really felt like I had finally got the hang of this Mathematics thing. In my excitement, I started to raise my voice, trying so hard to be noticed as one of the 'good' students concentrating. I'd end U*ncle Lanre's* sentences, cutting in *'yeah, yeah,' 'true,' 'that's right,' 'oh okay,'* a lot of times, and it began to look like I was the only one in the class. The Mathematics teacher wasn't having it anymore, so he cut in while I tried to make one of those interjections. *'You're not going to learn with the way you're doing,'* he spoke with a firmness that sounded like a rebuke. Ah, what now? Here I was, expressing joy that I actually feel good in a Mathematics class for the first time. *This tutor should be happy with himself he's doing a great job.*

As much as he was our tutor, I couldn't see him as more than a guy because he had no larger-than-life carriage of himself. He spoke less and often looked good in his well-ironed, native outfits. He wore prescription lenses and his wristwatches often matched his outfit. For a second, I felt deflated, quiet, and slightly embarrassed, but I could see the relief on everyone else's faces in the class. Like finally, someone had gotten the caution that she deserved! I took it all in and dedicated the remaining time in class to plotting how I'd get back at Uncle *Lanre* for the public insult and adding some injury on top. Couldn't he have ignored my childish behaviour? Well, let's not blame him too much. He didn't know where I was coming from.

I was sure of one thing, though—I was going to deal with him, at least, in the mildest way possible.

My mom had let me use her phone once in a while, and some of my friends had reached me on her number several times, though I didn't have full custody.

It was the period when MTN ran free midnight calls from 12:30 am to 4 am every day. Hence, I was awake most nights talking with my cousin, Ibukun Akinsiku, whom I had just met during the remembrance service of our great grandfather, Pa. Akinsiku, at our hometown, Ondo. It was an event that had brought us all together for the first time. I remember us dancing from Yaba to Lisaluwa and back to Fagun Estate, with portraits of our great grandfather. Some of us were in front while others followed the band behind in our coordinated *aṣọ ẹbi*—the prestigious *alari* and *sanmiyan,* popular among the Ondo people of Yoruba origin in Southwest Nigeria. We would have judged people in the same situation but here we were dancing off to praise and worship songs, not in honour of God, but of our dead ancestor. But we were happy doing it.

Ordinarily, we would complain that the sun was too scourging for such a long trek. Culture is really powerful. However, I believe that some cultural practices need to be modified if it is detrimental to the wellbeing of the observers. Thankfully, in our case, it was all fun and a bonding process for us great-grandchildren. That day, Ibukun, my cousin, and I connected quickly and kept in touch.

Since I was up most midnights on the phone with my cousin, an idea quickly struck my mind. I had *Uncle Lanre's* contact, so I was set to 'deal' with him. That morning, I started to call him on the dot at 12:30 am; I'd call and quickly hang up as he attempted to answer. I did that consecutively for about 30 minutes. In Nigeria, it is called *flashing*. It was my cousin Olawumi Taiwo, who first asked what *flashing* meant. 'Wumi couldn't understand when I had used it in the middle of a sentence, and she kept asking me to explain what it meant. In her deep American accent, *'what's a flash?' 'what's flashing?'*

Apparently, it was a Nigerian thing. How would someone pick up the phone and dial the other person only to hang up as soon as they attempt to answer? That's ridiculous unless you're in danger, and it's your last resort, right? My friend once tried it with her strict, no-nonsense, cleric father when she ran out of funds in school and needed to reach home. Instead of getting money, however, she got the scolding of her life. According to her dad, that was foolish behaviour, and she should have found a way to call, even if it meant borrowing. At that time, commercial phone call centres charged N20 per minute for calls.

Well, I flashed the hell out of *Uncle Lanre*. That time, people hadn't got the wisdom of switching off or barring unwanted numbers from calling them, so I simply stopped when I was done. I'd wait to hear his voice on the other end and quickly apply the red button. It felt fulfilling hearing his distressed voice, trying to figure out who was interrupting his sleep. And yes, I had hidden my number. How disturbing, annoying and frustrating. I feel so terrible now and would never be so vengeful again. I think it was my way of seeking justice for what I thought was unfair treatment. However, putting others in a place of distress is never the way to go. In retrospect, I could have spoken to him about how I felt after the class that day. He was approachable and a jolly good fellow. I'd later meet his two younger brothers, and they were amazing individuals. Sigh. I can now get the incident off my chest if this counts as a confession chapter.

Chapter Eight

My Friends and I

'Not everyone will be exposed to opportunities, but those who are, must share a portion with those who are not but are willing to put in some work.'

2010 was the beginning of so many things. However, two things stood out: the new decade and my first semester as an undergraduate of the Department of Political Science, University of Ibadan. The former would later become a source of controversy ten years later, in 2020, when people got into cyberwars over whether it was a new decade or not.

I volunteered with Toyosi Akerele's RISE Networks, a youth-based leadership initiative to raise and equip young people with effective leadership and governance skills. RISE Networks has, in recent times, evolved into a Learning, Research, and Work readiness hub focused on artificial intelligence and data science.

I attended the RISE annual leadership conference in 2009 as a volunteer. When my commercial ushering side hustle was in full swing, I worked as an event usher on many Saturdays. The pay was not as rewarding as the idea of actually dressing up and cat walking all over the event venue in high heels, attending to guests and making sure all went as smoothly as possible. However, if we got paid N3k-N5k per day, it was a good deal. I got most of my shoes with proceeds from the ushering services.

I decided to usher for free at this Annual Youth Conference. Oh, I admired Toyosi Akerele. Her name rang a bell even if you haven't heard it before. My mom was a super fan.

I remember during the dress rehearsal for the conference, one of the guys asked if I'd rather work with crowd control than protocol. I shrugged. Deep within, I was not sure I wanted to do that. I asked why he thought I was better for crowd control, and he said I looked tough. *lmao!* Well, I got that a lot. A classmate once told me no guy in the class dared ask me out because *them no born them well*. I'm not sure I have any advice for other women perceived as tough, but I know there's something about expressing your femininity and just being yourself instead of acting out other people's pre-recorded scripts. You do not have to shrink to be approved by anyone. Perception is often totally different from reality, and people who genuinely wish to connect with you will take their time. Everyone has blood running through their veins at the end of the day and we all defecate so don't *look at Uche's face*. If you like to date a lady, ask her out. My brother, stop being lily-livered pretending it's her hard face. The worst that would happen is that she says no. Rejection is part of life.

I did not join crowd control because this crowd was beyond control. The RISE youth conference was always a hit- a mix of young people genuinely young for growth and those simply at RISE Conference for the rice [or any other refreshment offered].
Toyosi Akerele would sit at the back of the hall, watching as everything went on. But once she spoke, the whole hall turned to see the woman behind that hefty, authoritative, almost intimidating voice. If confidence were a person, it would be her for me. I wanted so badly to be that confident and sure of who I was and wanted to be. Of course, I second guess once in a while because of the high standards I keep setting for myself, but I can only be glad I'm much more self-confident now than I was eleven years ago. A long walk to freedom.

A year later, it was the year preceding the general elections, so campaigns and electioneering processes had begun. Former President Goodluck Jonathan, who was initially the Vice President, was given constitutional powers by a federal court to carry out state affairs while his boss, the then president, Umar Musa Yar'Adua, was on medical treatment in a hospital in Saudi Arabia. Sadly, Yar'Adua didn't survive it. He later passed on 5th May, 2010, making Goodluck the substantial President of the Federal Republic of Nigeria. He then decided to run for office as President.

True to his name, many had ascribed former President Goodluck Jonathan's political fortune to sheer luck. Or how would one explain his emergence as Governor of Bayelsa State in 1998, when the State's Assembly impeached his boss, the then governor, Diepreye Alamieyeseigha, after being charged and found guilty of money laundering in the United Kingdom? Twelve years later, Goodluck took his boss's vacated job again.

A few months to the end of the tenure, Jonathan had indicated an interest in running for the Presidency. He enjoyed the goodwill of so many who perceived him as a complete gentleman with compassion and empathy. That's really a virtue missing in many leaders of this nation. If they really felt the pain of the masses, perhaps, it would push them to do better. This is not a declaration of my support for Jonathan's political affiliations or anything because, eventually, people-centered policies and their effective implementation determine good governance and not basic personal qualities of the leader.

Personality trait only plays a role. We must strive to build strong institutions that will birth effective succession and sustainable development. Even now, we have not begun to scratch the surface. If you do not believe, here are some key indicators of good governance: Rule of Law, Transparency and Accountability, Equity and Inclusiveness, Government Responsiveness, Effective Citizen Engagement, an enabling environment for citizens to flourish and Effective and Efficient Policy Formulation.

As part of his campaign activities, Goodluck Jonathan was launching a book, *My Friends and I,* a collection of his interactions and conversations on the popular social media platform *Facebook. Facebook* was relatively new, and many Nigerians were beginning to sign up. If I ever thought of myself as an elite or to be in the elite class, that text message inviting me for the launch of President Goodluck Jonathan's *My Friends and I* must have made me assume so.

"Dear Titi Oyeola, you have been invited to the official launch of 'My friends and I'
Venue: Eko Hotel and Suites, Victoria Island Lagos
Time: 10am
This event is strictly by invitation!"
I screamed. I just got an invite to see the President, bro! It was the sweetest feeling. *How did they get my number? Who sent this invite? Who*

knows me? I later got another text message from the RISE Networks asking me to confirm my attendance for the invitation. I wasted no time in responding, *yes!* Apparently, Rise Networks had been given some exclusive invites. They decided to share with their pool of volunteers. I was elated. All the payment we got volunteering was souvenirs and 'thank you' messages. But you see, such opportunities should never be reduced to cash rewards. The benefits outweigh financial gratifications, and I can tell you for free.

I arrived at Eko Hotel and Suites at about 10 am on the day. The atmosphere was rapturous. Students from highbrow schools in Lagos were invited.

When I saw a group of men dressed in black suits making coordinated steps towards the hall, I knew that power was not a joke. Mr. President was in the middle of these 40 men, I counted. He looked exactly like who we watched on the television. I quickly noticed that signature bowler hat but more unforgettably, the calm smile sitting pretty on his dark face. Mr. Goodluck Ebele Jonathan. I was happy; not many people get to see the President face to face. It was the same day I saw P-Square, popular twin music artists. I fell in love with them all over again. They had not gone solo at the time. Their hit song, *'Temptation'* featuring Alaye, was my caller tune for so many months. I loved the song so much I kept renewing. Peter and Paul looked so fresh you could almost bring out your tongue to lick their skin. But, of course, they were all guarded, and I didn't have a camera phone to request a selfie then.

Anyway, I have outgrown being star-struck over any celebrity. A B-list celebrity fresh off from Multichoice's *Big Brother* show taught me the hard lesson when he publicly snubbed me at a picnic in Agodi Gardens, Ibadan, where I had randomly run into him during Boxing Day hang out with some of my girlfriends, Omolola, Damilola and Toyyibah. It was crazy, but rather than feel embarrassed, I actually felt sorry for him because I am aware celebrity status does not confer superiority on anyone.

At Eko hotels, I saw a happy side of the country. — people randomly flexing, and no one was blinking because it was normal. You'd quickly forget the horrible statistics constantly being rolled out about the average Nigerian living below a dollar per day. I guess it depends on which side of the country you are because if care is not taken, some privileged citizens would continue to live in their own bubbles, under the illusion that things are not as bad.

The book launch deemphasized politicking but focused a lot on connecting with young people and helping them harness their capabilities. There were panel discussions and entertainment by popular Nigerian artists, but I can never forget lunch. We had joined a queue in another hall for lunch which was thoroughly organized. I thought only comfortable people could have been so well behaved. It was a buffet that had almost every food item in this world.

The concept of equality has always been hard for me to chew. But, at least, let every citizen be given their fundamental human rights. Embedded in these rights are the vital core of human security– access to basic healthcare, food, protection of lives and property of citizens, good road infrastructure, and access to basic social amenities. All these should be made available without any struggle, but sadly, this is not the case in Nigeria today. It is why some privileged individuals make a show of charity activities as if they are doing the world a favour. For example, they post pictures of the poor, thanking them for the food items that have been donated.

I cringe at such posts because without knowing, we are depriving these people of their humanity and every sense of self-worth just because they are victims of a failed system. However, if we must post these videos for information, let us endeavour to blur the faces of the beneficiaries just to help them retain some iota of their dignity, even if they are kids.

This experience formed part of *my* perspective about wealth and opportunities. Not everyone will be exposed to opportunities, but those who are must share a portion with those who are not but willing to put in some work. That describes how I found myself in Eko Hotel and Suites, Victoria Island, dining with the President.
Goodluck Jonathan later won that election in 2011 and was President till 2015 when he lost his second term bid to President Muhammadu Buhari, the candidate of the All Progressives Congress [APC].

Chapter Nine

Dear Daddy

...We see things the way we are, so for me, he was her father

I was hell-bent on going to the University of Ibadan. I thought it to be the best compensation for the long time I stayed home before securing admission into the university.

The University of Ibadan is said to be the first and the best among federal Universities in Nigeria, and I had waited so long to casually insert my academic affiliation with the citadel of learning into all my conversations: *'Oh, that's UI for you oh', 'Oh, they don't allow that in my school.'* I rehearsed how I would say these things so it could come out as natural as possible. Vanity!

Well, I got a shocker when school finally resumed after a six-month ASUU [Academic Staff Union of Universities] strike that began shortly after the admission notification. I was so discouraged. *Haba!* I waited three years for this badge of honour. I didn't deserve the delay, which I voluntarily blamed on the lecturers. Shouldn't they put the destiny of the students first? Shouldn't they take their job more seriously *abi kini gbogbo eleyii gannn?* [What is all these?] I was inconsolable and couldn't wait a day more. But when we do not assume a dispassionate analysis of issues, we argue for our own gain at all times. The strike actions have been a recurring phenomenon for so many decades in Nigeria. There needs to be a critical analysis of the situation if it must be effectively addressed. ASUU and the Federal Government are always dragging each other from *pòtòpótò* to *pòtòpótò*. This *pòtòpótò* [mud] is the failure of the government to adequately fund its institutions yet, pretend to be interested in innovation. A huge joke! This *pòtòpótò* has soiled the *ọpọlọ* [mental capacity] of *ọpọlọpọ* [so many]

54

students and lecturers. In fact, it has killed innovations and buried great ideas that would have been racing, like cheetahs, out of our institutions in rapid succession. The country appears like a joke to the rest of the world when its higher institutions are closed for sometimes as long as six to nine months for non-life-threatening reasons, like Covid -19, and which can be resolved if the government displays the amount of willingness that they profess loudly but clearly do not possess. My sympathy went up for the lecturers in Nigerian universities when a professor of repute lamented that his salary was less than a thousand dollars. This cannot be justifiable in a country with a wasteful bi-cameral legislature, where lawmakers smile home with over N13.5 million monthly, after merely warming the benches in the green and red chambers. Yet, the people saddled with knowledge production and transmission are left to wallow in poverty.

It is not surprising that we have remained a third world country, not even on its way to moving up the ladder of development. Imagine the government negotiating university resumption after months of needless closure—such a shame. Yet, a whopping sum of N37 billion was earmarked for the renovation of the National Assembly chambers in 2020. The roofs of the chambers were caught licking in June 2021. This is the part where we all throw up, right?

Let us face it, the educational system is sinking by the day, and that's putting it mildly, but what do we expect? I have passed through the university a second time now, and it is clear that things are taking a backward spiral movement. The government's arrogant breach of contract precipitates interruptions in academic processes, making it difficult for the higher institutions to play their role of bridging the gap between the gown [academic research] and the town [the rest of society]. Why do we have so many institutions with so little innovation? Many lecturers in Nigerian institutions are now reduced to 'hustlers' due to the government's failure. There is a clear division of interest, and you won't blame them. They have families. *Who research epp?* These are the issues – the *koko*.

In anticipation of the good news that the ASUU strike had been called off, I stuck more to the 'News at 9' and every other news channel that there was. I joined my mom to listen to *Tifun Tedo*, a Yoruba news program that tends to exaggerate issues in a way that made it both fun and engaging.

'Folake ooooo,' the co-presenter would call, and Folake would respond with an exaggerated urgency. It was usually comic relief each time. I enjoyed it over other news sources because the news about ASUU's resumption would sound different and sweeter coming from the duo of Folake Otuyelu and Kola Ladoke or Bayo Faleke.

My expectations had been so high of the premier university because it had to reflect this adjective in every sense of the word. Fun fact I had decided it was the University of Ibadan that day in Primary Five when my school took us on an excursion to the zoological garden. The students looked like 'gods,' so decent, so posh. Some of them even said, 'Hi' to us, and we looked at them with so much adoration.

Hmmm, my people, it took the registration process to shake the initial *gra gra* off my body. I was devastated. How can things be this rigorous, *nitori ọlọrun?* [For God's sake]. Only a little part of the registration process was automated. A lot of the steps were manual, and you had to join endless queues with thousands of other students parked like sardines in front of an office, trying to sign one document or another. It was so stressful that students picked numbers on different queues and would quickly head to the one with a closer number, and sadly, before they were back to the other queue, the attendant had closed their window.

'Come back tomorrow,' they'd yell as though they were doing you a favour and not their job. Some students, out of frustration, would burst out in tears. That's how you identified the 'freshers' [new students] from the stalelites [returning students]. Some would start begging the attendant and even come up with a lie about their Genotype. *'Excuse me ma, I have sickle cell disorder and can't stand for long.'* It fell on deaf ears. Left to those attendants, *problem ti ẹ nìyẹn* [That's your problem].

It shocked me to realise that accommodation was not automatically provided upon admission into the university. I can never forget the daily nightmarish shuffle between registration and the struggle for accommodation. I was allocated to Queen Elizabeth II Hall, one of the two female hostels owned by the university. But, unfortunately, the allocation was one thing, 'long leg' was another.

I'm a firm believer in building institutions and not sabotaging the system for personal gain. However, the Nigerian system often forces innocent citizens to act against stipulated rules like almost everybody else. If a new student gets an allocation to a certain hall of residence, does that not imply that a space has been reserved for the student there? However, the students get allocation officially, yet were left stranded when they realise that apart from students with special needs, medical students in premed school and a few other highly connected students, others have to find their way despite being officially allocated to the hall of residence.

Despite priding myself as a good citizen, I succumbed to finding my way too. I pressed a few 'buttons' and got an accommodation. But this was after several weeks of standing on the 200-500 body-long queues and endlessly circling out of sight of the goal, an office door soon to close for lunch alongside thousands of other prospective occupants. I tried. It was such a relief finally getting allocated to H27.

The campus life often sends a pleasant taste down my throat. It did not look exactly like what I envisaged, but it was not horrible. The first thing that caught my attention was how many girls, different, yet the same, in many ways, flocked in and out of Queen Elisabeth II Hall gate. Of course, the university will show you all sorts of people. But one thing common was that we all had questions on our faces that we hoped would be answered by academic or other means.

We quickly developed a sense of commonality because when six girls live in one room, I guarantee they had no choice. My hostel had nine blocks of buildings, and I had expected a haven, given the perception circulated about the first female hostel in the University. But we met a downgraded version. We were not served chicken and jollof every Sunday as our parents, and we had to stand long queues, more queues, to get water on some occasions. There was no 24 hours' electricity supply.

A lot of occupants had squatters because many could not secure a hostel accommodation. It was better for the male students than for the female students, seeing there were about six male hostels and one mixed hostel to only two female hostels. Squatting often happened despite the strong directive against the act. Some rooms with six occupants still managed to allow an extra bunkie with a stern warning that the information remained unshared with non-occupants.

Oftentimes, one struggles to know the actual owner of a bed space. Bunks were carefully arranged in horizontal, linear forms leaving only a tiny portion for movement across the room. I wonder how we survived such sardine-like squash of an arrangement. It got better from 300 Level. Only two to three students were allocated to a room. Some squatters were badly behaved while many simply respected themselves. One day, a student was caught stealing a pack of unused recharge cards which belonged to an occupant in the next room. Girls had found a way to access certain commodities without having to go all the way to the buttery close to the entrance of the hostel. Recharge cards were sold on almost every floor. The stolen pack was found with this young lady, who later confessed to squatting in one of the rooms.

My heart sank as she was paraded to the porters' lodge as if to make a criminal statement against herself. Beautiful, tall, dark with skin shining-like glass; I could have sworn it would never be her in such a mess. Well, hers was one of several theft cases. Yet, we carried ourselves as queens because one bad egg cannot come and spoil our shine.

We were happy—freedom of sorts and dreams, not all academic, given the opportunity to come true. One of the major highlights of the hostel life was The Hall Week. It was an annual observation packed with series of activities, and the Hall Dinner was the grand finale. As girls, we went over and beyond to find the perfect dinner dress, and of course, a partner. Mhen, the pressure! *Wahala for who no get boyfriend o. Double wahala for who no get fine boyfriend o.* Girls went as far as renting a fine boy as their dinner date just to 'pepper' other girls who had planned to steal the show as usual. There was competition about who wore the best dress and we would long for a *'Oh, your dress is so lovely,'* compliment or spend the rest of the night wallowing in buyer's remorse over spending your whole month's allowance on that skimpy dress from Preboyes.

Preboyes sits temptingly at the main highway junction leading to Bodija market adjacent the university gate. Any resident of Queens Hall that didn't patronize Preboyes World Boutique was not considered boogie at all. The boutique had every 'big girl's' outfit, and the higher the price, the higher the quantity demanded. If you mentioned that you bought your dress and shoes from Preboyes, your value would go up a notch in the eye of the happening babes. *You sef don belong be that.*

It was the night when girls legit let their hair down, unlike those times they sneaked out to nightclubs a few minutes before twelve since the hostel and university gates were closed at midnight. I remember how certain modes of dressing were frowned upon so girls who went out on Friday nights to parties or nearby clubs would wear a robe over their outfit to deceive the hostel porters who often policed them loco parentis.

I didn't feel pressured to attend night clubs because it seemed like a lot of work the morning after when my roommate and friends would spread themselves on the bare floor, worn-out to their bones from waist shaking activities all night. *Is this what clubbing looks like? I no come dis life to suffer, abeg.* So, I stuck with intellectually stimulating activities. At least, one must be known for something. I decided to be my Hall's Public Relations Officer. Victoria Osuji, in her soft, yet firm voice, would make announcements via the public address system at the porters' lodge. *'Dear Queens, this is the voice of the PRO,'* and go on to pass a piece of information. I loved that part of being the PRO. I rehearsed in preparation for my turn. It came in 200 Level when I contested and won. My opponent was Chioma from the Faculty of Arts. It was a landslide victory. I wish I had a conversation with her about how she handled the loss because I can only imagine.

The entrance of Queen II Hall had a beautiful night view. It was a perfect hang out spot for many students who came visiting their friends in the hostel or girls seeing off their boyfriends who had come visiting. Male students were allowed in between 4 pm and 9 pm. There were often pairs of students standing or sitting on the edge of the pavement in conversations. I was surprised when I sighted my fellowship's former President one night, sitting with a female member. Both of them were in an intense conversation that came with blushing smiles seen by teeth reflecting the passing light of nearby cars.

So, pastors too fall in love? *Nawa o.* It felt strange because many fellowship leaders were adored as though they were not students. They were prohibited from many regular activities. What a huge sacrifice this set of people made to ensure the sustainability of spiritual activities within the campus. I thought they overdid it sometimes, especially when one time, the *mama* walked up to me that my earrings were too bold for a worker and I needed to watch the length of my skirts. The *mama* is the Sisters' Coordinator of the fellowship, often revered in the status of the wife of the General Overseer of a church.

To think that I prided myself as modest enough, I wore short skirts a lot but never too short for a University undergraduate. It didn't help matters that her room was just next to mine. The rules were a lot and could have encouraged hypocrisy because many of the leaders soon went back to their usual student lifestyle immediately after they handed over to another person. You could sometimes see the sigh of relief and a different level of cheerfulness on their faces. Many of the guys went on to marry the ladies they criticized as too flashy or seductive in the fellowship. Hmm, *e choke!*

....

My only experience of a nightclub happened in the day. It was a Departmental Freshers' Orientation that ended with an excursion. We had been taken on a tour around major places in Ibadan. It was helpful for students who came from outside the town, even though some of the resident students had not been to a few of the places visited. For instance, it was my first visit to *Láyípo. Láyípo* is believed to be the centre of the ancient city, '*Ẹ̀bá Ọ̀dàn,*' known today as Ibadan. There is hardly any place in Ibadan without a rich historical lyric.

The Bower's Tower, popularly known as *Láyípo,* was unveiled in December 1936. The 60ft tall tower was named after Captain Robert Lister Bower, the first British Resident in the city of Ibadan. The tower earned the name *Láyípo* from its 47 spiral staircase, which implies that climbers would have to ascend the hill in a spiral format, which, in Yoruba, is translated as *Láyípo.* Located at the foot of Bẹẹrẹ area of the city of Ibadan, indigenes often adopted a lyric of welcome to visitors. They would chant '*Ọmọ Ibadan, oòmọ Láyípo.*' It means if you do not know *Láyípo,* then you have not been to Ibadan.

That hill gives a clear view of major buildings such as Trenchard Hall, the Glass House, Cocoa House in Dugbe, University College Hospital and Cultural Centre in Mokola. It was such a pleasant view. The last time I visited Bowers' Tower, I almost shed tears because the place had taken a nose dive from my initial visit in 2010. The environment was deserted except for a few commercial motorbike operators who struggled to recall the place, and thick grasses had covered a larger part of the walking path that led to the 60 feet tall tower.

I made an attempt to interview the gatekeeper, who reluctantly told me that the place was not open every day anymore and he had only come on that day as a weekly ritual. I felt hurt that the government could be missing such a golden opportunity at economic prosperity for the State through tourism. Despite renovations conducted on the tower, it is yet to be optimized for revenue generation to the State. The States must explore more creative areas such as tourism to increase revenue generation because there is evidence that taxation alone cannot lead a State to prosperity and less dependence on the Federal Government's monthly allocation.

We concluded our excursion that day at a club. I had heard the name of the club before, but I had never been there. The lights dimmed at 7 pm, and all caution was thrown in the air. I could not even stand any guy caressing my body while we danced, so I sat still from the beginning till the end. I must have marveled at the strange activities that took place but it was strange only to me, the complete '*get inside child*' that I was.

I became friends with a few guys who confessed their respect for me went a notch higher after that night. Were they saying they lost respect for the other girls who danced with them? Can you imagine them judging the girls who agreed to dance with them? Why should the subject of respect or otherwise be directed only at the ladies in such cases? I see it that two adults agree to keep each other's company on the dance floor so if their conducts amount to moral decadence, then both should lose respect not just the lady.

......

One of the events that stuck with me during my stay at the university happened one Friday morning. It should have been a regular occurrence that anyone would overlook but I couldn't because it triggered deep, painful emotions that I had unconsciously repressed. Even now, I am not sure if I am done healing. It reminded me of 'daddy'. When I was younger, I made up stories about my daddy taking my siblings and I on a trip or buying us chocolate and whatnot when my classmates said same of theirs after a few weeks of vacation. The pressure to have a daddy too, was so much I had to make up stories. But as I grew up, I realized I was actually lying to myself so I painfully embraced my reality. I'd imagine what my dad would do in certain situations, especially when I was in trouble and needed someone to protect me.

My dad was a fantastic man. He was never serious about spiritual activities because he had read everything in Sight-Philosophy, Spiritual Literature, Political books, Activism and so forth. He loved Fela Anikulapo-Kuti and I remember him and my mother having regular disagreement over his obsession for anything *abamiẹda* [a strange human]. I loved my father so much and I admired his empirical mindset. I was however worried that whenever my mom urged him to join family prayers, he'd brush it off and make jokes about how no one could be after his life because he was not MKO Abiola! Despite his unchristian way of life, he cared for his kids and he was the finicky parent who ensured our socks was spotless every day. On many evenings, he paid us some coins to scratch his back for him. He'd carry me on his shoulder and I suspect I could have been his favourite child since I was the only one born in his presence. Maybe I'm just trying to console myself since everyone seemed taken but me. My sister was clearly everybody's favourite —all gifts from family members abroad were boldly labelled in her name. My older brother, being the first son obviously had a special place in my mom's heart and I often told her. My younger brother, of course, the baby of the house had his own special privileges because he got away with many things I wouldn't have dared. All that left me stranded and always struggling for attention. What's that thing about middle child identity crisis? Ọmọ, it's so real.

Whatever sweet memories I have of my dad ended when I was about six or seven years old. He became someone else. My parents could no longer be together and the family took a new turn. I prayed and fasted a lot for a miracle, that one day. I'd be back from school to the most pleasant surprise that daddy was back home. But it never happened. I felt like God broke my heart and I carried that hurt for years. I missed my father and wished we could be in touch but by the time that happened, it was too late. I was already an adult and we had grown too wide apart.

******

I was going to pay my fees in Afribank [now Polaris Bank] next to the university's main gate. I planned to dedicate the whole day to that activity because paying school fees was more than just walking into the bank and remitting cash; a different, avoidable and tedious process was attached. The queue was crazy because everyone somewhat felt it was safer to use the bank closest to the school in case there was a technical issue which was usually a regular case. Luckily, I never had any. God knows I couldn't stand such stress!

Some security agents in police uniforms were hanging around the banking hall if any student misbehaved. I guess experience had taught them to beef up security. It was getting late for a Friday when many people shut down from work any time past 1 pm, partly for Islamic prayers and mostly out of mere indulgence. I didn't want to be held down at the bank, seeing I still had to go into the school's administrative department for some update of the teller issued at the bank.

I was getting worked up and frustrated, but the security men had instructed us not to move past a certain line, which I thought was unfair seeing some people were still gaining access. *Do they have two heads?* I simply crossed the line following a fair-skinned, 5.6-ish tall young lady, who I presumed was not a fresh student because she had broken the rule so confidently with no one stopping her. Going in with her sounded like a smart idea, or not! One police officer came over and yelled at me, *'Hey, what are you doing there!'* or something like that. I went mum, too nervous to say anything. It wasn't just me after all; let the other girl respond. *Ọmọ*, to my greatest surprise, he bundled both of us out of the premises and was about to arrest us. For real! Police brutality takes various forms and indeed, the Police has not rebranded from its initial mandate when established in the 1860's. The Nigeria Police Force was established by the British colonial authorities to protect the British colonial administrators, not Nigerians. The colonialists needed protection from the local communities who resisted colonial rule and in response, the Nigeria Police was created and the officers were paid stipends. There must really be a total, thorough and deliberate Police Reform. Mandate, remuneration, and other critical issues must be addressed.

The law enforcement agents have to do better. Even if we were criminals, we deserved some dignity and fair treatment. We had indeed done wrong by jumping the queue, but they shouldn't strip us of our humanity because of that. He said we broke the rule and were going to be punished by the school authority *bla bla bla*. I started to cry, perhaps, to invoke pity because I was so tired of all the hassle. The other lady kept a straight face, chewing gum and rolling her eyes. One would wonder where she got that confidence from, but I would soon find out because as we walked towards the exit gate, a black Lexus Jeep was parked right in front of the metal signpost that read *'No Parking.'* It was tinted, so we couldn't see through, but as we moved closer, the driver rolled down and in the backseat was a man I figured would be in his early 50's. He had barely uttered any word but I knew there was something about him I mean, who breaks the *No Parking* rule with their full chest like that? In this country, only a big woman or man would.

The lady kept walking fast towards him, and for some reason, I followed her. This man could probably save us from the mess we got in. I was wrong; he only had plans to save his daughter! *What happened?* he inquired in a powerful Igbo accent. By then, the policemen were shivering. They suddenly went quiet, and that made me happy. When Nigerians come across a wealthy or powerful person, they quickly start to chant, *'Well-done ma, well-done sir,'* as though they believe the individual must have been really busy making money. These policemen did not prove me wrong. *'oga well-done O, we dey loyal.'* The man said no word but only beckoned at one of the policemen. I wonder what transpired, but the girl was escorted back into the banking hall to carry out her transaction. I stood there helpless, angry, but most importantly, completely broken.

It was one of the many days I missed having a father. I'm not sure that was her father, but he protected her, and that was all that mattered. It could be he was making sure his money was actually used to pay the fees and not disappearing into his daughter's hand bag or the latest human hair. He could have been anything else to her-an uncle, a lover, man friend or *sugar daddy*. But we see things the way we are, so for me, he was her father.

Chapter Ten

When Good Men Do Nothing
'The only thing necessary for the triumph of evil is for good men to do nothing'-Edmund Burke.

My first encounter with Ajibola Adigun was at the Student's Legislative Council Meeting. I had been elected to represent the 100 Level Constituency while he was representing 200 Level. He was only a year ahead of me, but I'd later find out he was several miles ahead of many in intellect.

'This argument does not hold water,' Ajibola affirmed during screening of new Executive Council members and an audit of how the annual dues were expended. In Political Science Department, we operated a Presidential model where a Senate performed checks and balances duties, and then the Executive, comprised the President and her/his Cabinet members. The elected President recommends members of her/his cabinet, and the Senate then screens these proposed cabinet members. It is the same system operated by the Federal Government of Nigeria.

On that day, the Senate debated how the President, Jamiu Adebayo, my good friend to date, performed during his reign as President of the Departmental Association.

I had carefully prepared to make a statement at this seating because what is the point of all the big grammar when the whole place was littered by the same people who blame the government for everything? You can't even clean up or dispose of your trash properly! Goodluck Jonathan couldn't have been the only problem *abeg*. So, I raised my hand and the Senate President, authorised me to speak. I nervously rushed my point as I thought it was a bit off the point of discussion and odd that I had to come up with such an 'insignificant' issue in the middle of a heated conversation. It was still important. Littering is an issue, even in our society today. Many people still throw out garbage from their car on the high way and some load their trunks with luggage to dispose at unauthorised dumpsites, culverts and roadsides. Please stop it! Maybe no one paid attention, but I did, and it's why I do not litter to date. I'll always find the closest waste bin or keep a waste paper in my bag until I can dispose of it appropriately. I really would rather litter my bag than the streets.

After the seating, I quickly walked up to Jibola. I knew I had to be his friend. This guy was loaded. For me, I never just sit and admire anyone from afar; I simply walk up and strike a conversation. It didn't matter if you were female or male. I once did that with Adetoke, whom I met at Global Harvest Church choir rehearsal for the first time. It was a supercharged atmosphere with top-notch singers; swag *ti poju*. This was [and is still] a star-studded choir full of the best vocalists in town. *Oporrr*. '*I'm here for it all*,' I thought to myself. Adetoke was a breath of fresh air that day. She seemed very relaxed and laid back in the middle of everyone else singing their throats out, trying to get their harmonies right. It was real work, but she appeared in control and unmoved. That got me fascinated. I didn't hesitate to reach out.

I had struck a conversation with Jibola in the same manner, and we couldn't seem to stop. So I asked how he could construct such beautiful grammatical expressions. His response was a broad smile that told me he was flattered but not surprised. So often, many people had commended him for the same. We became, and are still very good friends.

....

Faculty elections were usually such fun. Different factions and build up towards Election Day brought a high adrenaline rush for both the contestants and their supporters. I was never much interested in faculty politics, but I later became the information Minister of my department in my final year.

Ajibola was contesting for the Presidency after much persuasion from supporters who found him very intelligent and someone who had a lot to offer. He had reluctantly agreed, and a group of friends gathered more supporters, one of which I was supposed to be. Apart from being friends, we bonded over debate contests where we represented the

Department in inter-university contests, winning all categories for the Department.

Suffice to say it never got to Ajibola that I usually emerged Best Speaker all of the time. He was that confident an individual. So, it was a no brainer that I supported him, but there came a huge BUT - Jibola Suara, a friend of my friend, Elisabeth Ebunoluwa Ezekiel, was contesting for the same position. So, I was torn between two 'Jibola' worlds. Elisabeth, being the super strong-willed babe, had quickly expressed her decision to both of them. She would simply not vote since she was friends with both contestants. I, on the other hand, remained on the fence. I'd later experience a harrowing fall off that fence.

Campaigns started in full swing, and I displayed background support for Jibola Adigun. I wasn't so close with Jibola Suara, but you see, when it comes to politics, it's not often so easy to take a side; Power changes people, and the quest for it can reveal the true nature of those you thought you knew. But that didn't change the fact that I wasn't bold enough to take a stand. I didn't go all out for my friend. I could have used my influence as the popular debater to garner support, but I went underground. I became a spectator where I should have been a gladiator.

On the eve of the election, there had been rumours that some supporters removed campaign posters of opponents and Jibola Adigun was affected. It hurt me further that I ran into a couple of his supporters trying to conduct last-minute campaigns that night, but I kept walking, wishing it all away. The emotional baggage, the '*I should have*' worsened when I finally saw him on the other side of the football field where they talked with a group of fresh students. My heart sank, not out of hypocrisy, but the feeling of guilt that I could have been there for a friend and it was rather too late. I simply walked over with an emotional baggage I could have shed earlier by simply taking a side.

The next day, Jibola Adigun called me to say he lost the election as if I hadn't heard. His words stuck to me like glue. It sounded like a paraphrase of a popular quote ascribed to Edmund Burke. -The only thing necessary for the triumph of evil is for good men to do nothing. I'll never forget. That day, I learnt to never sit on the fence on issues that matter to me. It was cowardice to do so. Both Jibolas became great friends, and Adigun is one friend I'll always hold in high esteem.

Chapter Eleven

Hello Idumota
'...Rather, we chose people pleasing, needless stress and outright self-endangerment.'

Although I was born in Lagos, the most I know about the city is how it has everything you want: clothing, electronics, household items, especially people. Of its many nicknames, *eko wenjele* always stood out for me. It sounded like a warning not to let your guards down or allow yourself to get swindled. Eko must be *wenjele* indeed because we never went out except to school and church. We attended the National Headquarters of the Foursquare Gospel Church in Yaba. I'll never forget waking up early to make the services after a very long drive from our home on John Olugbo Street, Ikeja. There were closer branches, but something about the headquarters made it our first choice, distance regardless. My mom had also influenced her disciple, Uncle Dapo Aderibigbe and family, to attend the Headquarters so it was a principle for her than mere paparazzi of big church branches. Mama Abby [*name changed*] gave us a ride in her white Volkswagen, old model beetle car. The one Yoruba people call *'ijapa'* because it has the shape of a tortoise. So tiny, it looked exactly like its owner. Petite, plump, fair-skinned, South/South woman, Mama Abby was a handful. She always complained about everything but herself. However, my mom and her found a way to get along. I never liked her; none of my siblings did. So, we all grumbled when we heard the loud noise from her honking; it sounded rude. *Mama Tolu! Mama Tolu!* She'd yell from the entrance of our gate. I wished my mom could tell her off one of those days, but she didn't. See, if you ever quarrel with my mother, you're at fault.

Ladylak was the children department of Foursquare National Headquarters, and we mostly sang lyrical adaptations from Bible characters.

'Read your Bible pray every day…
pray every day…, pray every day…
Read your Bible pray every day…
If you want to grow.'

Then, there was my favourite

'I have joy down in my heart,
deep deep down in my heart.
J.O.Y down in my heart,
deed deep down in my heart.'

The way we used our hands to draw the J.O.Y sign brought some believability to the concept of Joy. Our faces would light up each time the song got to the joy part. Children are so innocent in a sweet way.

We spent the whole Sunday in church. From Ladylak, we moved to the main church. There was always one activity: holy communion, thanksgiving service, Annual General Membership meeting, Baptismal Class, something. I could never understand why we had to spend so much time in church. The concept of worship has been modified especially with the coronavirus pandemic. It is essential to understand that activity and relationship with God are two different sides of a coin, and one must not be mistaken for the other. We might have been compelled to participate in the activities that kept us so long in church premises, but I am thankful that as we grew, we also found time to establish and maintain a relationship with God, our maker.

Years later, people talk about places in Lagos and expect I'd contribute since I once lived there. Well, as you can see, we were *get-inside* kids. But I really wanted to explore those places - Idumota, Balogun, and Oyingbo, the commercial heartbeats of the Centre of Excellence.

****

I now know why I quickly agreed to go with Aminat Adeyemo to Idumota. Aminat was the Chairperson of Queen Elizabeth II, our Hall of residence in the University of Ibadan, while I was Public Relations Officer. The usual practice was that residents contributed an annual levy and got customised souvenirs in return. It was compulsory, as was the practice in the Departments and Faculties. The EXCO would determine the souvenir items based on the amount contributed. It, however, had to be commensurate with the amount paid or be ready to hear stories about how you used their money to buy yourself the latest phone or your new car.

We had decided to get tissue towels, a diary and a key holder, if I remember clearly. After careful consultations, we concluded that Lagos was the destination for the variety we needed at a highly reduced bulk price. Well, if you're buying over three thousand units of different items, you had better go to Lagos.

We headed for Idumota that morning: Aminat and I. We rode in the Student Union bus as the executive members were also making a trip to Lagos that day. It was my second official trip with the hall chairperson as the first was a courtesy visit to Afe Babalola [SAN] at his Afe Babalola University, Ado-Ekiti. He was an absolute delight to be around and I remember he asked each of us for our grades and encouraged us to always put in our best as students and as leaders. I was looking forward to the almighty Idumota. But, the truth is I couldn't tell my mom because I wasn't ready to hear how a woman was crushed by a moving trailer while negotiating with a roadside trader or how area boys snatched someone's bag and stabbed their wrist in the process. Moms always have one scary story or another.

The journey to Lagos was enjoyable, and we chatted away for the most part.
From Oshodi, a bus took us straight to Idumota after we parted ways with the student union crew. Idumota was buzzing.
Although there was a sense of urgency in the faces of every commuter, it wasn't as crazy as had been reported. Honestly, I thought I'd see people walking with their heads, but there were none.

We found a store that had all we wanted. Before anything, two elderly women were already shadowing us. It later occurred to me that they were *alabaaru* – labourers who lift buyers' goods from inside the market to their cars. I was looking around a lot, trying to catch a glimpse of the almighty Idumota market where everything happened, according to people. The trip was more of an excursion for me, and I'm glad Aminat had been the mother hen, cautioning me to focus each time I got carried away staring at older women graciously carrying heavy loads on their heads and pulling another in their hand while miraculously and magnificently managing to maintain an upright posture.

Though it worried me, their coordinated steps were so beautiful to watch. It looked like an elegant catwalk, as captivating as any fashion runway. I feared something could happen, and the load would pour. But it didn't. They had superbly mastered the art of properly positioning heavy items in the middle of their heads. They are *alabaaru*. They hardly bargained. They simply trusted their clients to reward them appropriately with a fee commensurate to the size of the goods they have carried for them. I wonder how the market would fare without these women.

Two of these women had carried our mass purchase. They, however, had to lift in batches because of the volume. Aminat stayed in front to lead them to a place we had secured to offload as we waited to hire a bus while I walked behind. 'Trust no one at the market' was the watchword. We had made two rounds and were on the third when we suddenly couldn't locate one of the women. We searched everywhere, but no one looked like her. As a matter of fact, all those *alabaaru* really looked alike, and you could only tell them apart by what they were carrying. For over an hour, we kept searching. Aminat was already in tears. Mine didn't even flow as much as I tried. We started imagining the worst. *Maybe she had gone away with the remaining goods. Maybe she missed her way but couldn't she have simply gone back to the store? Maybe she had connived with the store owner to dupe us since we appeared like novices.* Too many maybes and it was getting dark.

Traders were locking their stores, and the market traffic was getting leaner. The woman we put the stuff with advised us to leave as soon as possible because it was dangerous to be there at night, according to her. Of course, we knew, but leaving without finding the woman meant a debt to the tune of at least a hundred thousand Naira for us both. Somehow, I thought Aminat could get the money because of her posh campaign into the chairperson position she held. But how do we even open our mouths to say it? The other EXCO members would never believe us. They'd think we made it up. A whole us! Imagine.

After combing the market to no avail, we decided to leave. Call it a miracle, it must have been, but lo and behold, the *alabaaru* woman showed up. See, we almost tore her apart. *Kilosele, nibo le ya si, seko si any* problem, *[where have you been, was there any problem?]* we bombarded her with questions, but all she could mutter was gibberish. Only God knows what happened. We couldn't care, as long as goods were intact.

It was already about 7 pm, and we were left with the task of getting ourselves back to Ibadan or finding a place to pass the night since it was clearly too late to start travelling. All that didn't cross our minds earlier, and we were under a strict budget. It wasn't our money, for crying out loud. We got a *danfo* drop, and in my mind, a drop meant an exclusive ride where no other passenger is picked. I lied. This greedy conductor kept calling in passengers, so it ended up a normal commercial ride, only we were still made to pay the initially negotiated amount.

As if that wasn't enough, the driver suddenly pulled over and said he was no longer taking our route. Maybe he heard word that there was gridlock, so he took a last-minute decision. That means pulling all the sacks of goods out and standing by the road to find another bus. Thankfully, we found one to get us to Oshodi. Hmm, my mom's voice was ringing in my head. Standing at the centre of Oshodi at 9 pm waiting for a bus to Ibadan, was a real storm in a teacup. I knew it was dangerous, but it was our last resort. Aminat's parents-in-law to-be lived on the Island or so, and even if we made attempts to go there, we would still arrive at midnight. Besides, she and her boyfriend had been quarrelling the whole time because he blamed her for not carrying him along enough on the journey, or he'd have stepped in with a better plan. Meanwhile, my then-boyfriend fell fast asleep shortly after I messaged him to say that we had arrived in Oshodi. How dare he sleep!! I fumed. I stood by the motor park with the luggage while Aminat went to inquire if another bus was leaving for Ibadan that night. Some other passengers gathered around, and one of the drivers decided to move. We quickly arranged ourselves into the 14-seater bus, and it zoomed off.

One of the passengers had come to Lagos for a party and got held up in traffic. Her husband kept calling to find out where we'd reached, not without inserting some curse words into their conversation. *Aláìnísẹ́ oníṛinkùrin òṣì, torii oúnjẹ́ o gbéra lọ sí party ràdàràda ti wọn ò péè sí [A jobless woman who, because of a plate of food, took off to a party uninvited].* I felt sorry for the woman who kept pleading with her husband that it wasn't her fault that there had been such heavy traffic. Another passenger was a young lady who left Lagos without informing anyone at home and her family was calling to find out where she was. A man later picked her up at the toll gate at past midnight after the driver parked to continue the journey in the morning. Others were traders who came in to buy wholesale items in Lagos.

The tollgate has a very distinct nightlife. It was bubbling when one would expect the opposite. One roadside vendor was just setting up her Jollof rice stand. She had a huge pot full of jollof rice and a bucket by the side containing beef and fried chicken. There were alcohol vendors, palm wine, and mostly edible stuff. If there were no buyers, the vendors wouldn't be there.

We were too tired to panic, plus the blasting of loud music by the local make-do Disc Jockey eased off the tension anyone was bringing from wherever they were coming. I thought it wise to inform my older brother that I was cooling off at the toll gate. He was the only one who could handle it. My mom and sister would have high blood pressure thinking of what could go wrong; their daughter and sister passing the night in the custody of area boys. But it wasn't that bad after all. The night economy at the toll gate is something that should be studied, albeit dangerous these days

We spent the next day sleeping and gratefully reliving all that had transpired. We were tired, emotionally and physically. When I tried to fight him over his 'irresponsible' sleeping, my then-boyfriend [we later broke up!] thought we brought it all upon ourselves. We could have planned better. We had options, but we chose to be messiahs. He was right.

If you ask me, we could have:
1. Outsourced the purchase of items and attached a strict budget
2. Found a moderate hotel to pass the night
3. Hired a bus to and fro
4. Bought everything in Ibadan, *patapata* it would cost a bit more!

Rather, we chose people-pleasing, needless stress and outright self-endangerment.

Chapter Twelve

One Night Stand in the City of Rocks
Endless accusations would have dominated the conversation,
and we would end up regretting we ever spoke about it

'*Of course, I'd love to,*' I responded to Yomi [name changed]. Yomi was a temporary staff of Osun State Broadcasting Corporation, *Oke Baale*, Osogbo, where I observed my compulsory one-year National Youth Service Corps. He spoke with me about anchoring a TV show for kids. That sounded great. I was already doing newspaper reviews and reading the news on the radio, but I'd never been on Television except for one morning at work when a guest failed to show up for a segment on the breakfast show, and I had to become the makeshift guest. The focus was tertiary Education in Nigeria, and, sadly, the position I took back then is solid as a rock even now.

I suggested that having a foreign education puts the student at an advantage over studying solely in Nigeria because the educational quality needed an overhauling. Also, studying abroad provides a better level of exposure and understanding of diversity. At the same time, I stuttered to make my point because every statement is censored with a state-owned broadcasting channel, or you run into trouble with the powers-that-be. How can you be saying the people paying your bills are failing? Civil servants are compelled to be loyal to a government that fails to perform its basic duties. A government that fails to pay the salaries of its st
aff but demands the staff to sing its praises. How hypocritical.

Can we even talk about pensions? How can a citizen work for the government for 35 years, which are their main productive years, only for greedy politicians to swindle their retirement funds? It is wild, unbelievable.

Albeit, I made myself clear. The educational system was not and is not working in 2021. I don't know of the coming years. We just might witness a turnaround for the better.

Anyway, Yomi recommended me to the facilitators of the TV show that would air on a television station in Abeokuta, Ogun State. It was a paid gig, and we would get accommodation for the days when recording would last.

Although we didn't necessarily agree on modalities, it already sounded like a good idea, so I brought in another corps member and friend of mine who was also serving at the corporation. Princess was a set ahead of me, and we worked together at the News and Current Affairs Department.

It was the day before the shoot day. I already mentioned to my mom, out of excitement, that her daughter would be on TV. Although something was off; all day, we didn't receive any message about movement and meeting points. All we knew was that the recording was taking place the following day. I started to call George [not real name], the guy in charge; but his line was either off or he'd refuse to pick up when it went through. Princess was coming from Lagos, where she had spent the weekend, and I had planned to stop by at Ibadan before heading to Abeokuta the following day. I arrived in Ibadan at about 6 pm and stopped by somewhere to see a friend.

By now, George hadn't answered his call, and my mom had left a stern warning that it was too late to travel even if he eventually answered. Also, I wouldn't have left Osogbo if I knew the whole thing was a scam. So, I began to suspect Yomi since he also didn't have anything concrete to tell me when it was tough reaching George. He seemed so unconcerned it annoyed me. By the way, as stipulated in the Service Corps guidelines, Corps members were placed under travel restrictions during the period of service, so we only left on due permission from our temporary employers.

The next morning, George called with some flimsy excuse that didn't hold water, but I overlooked it So, Princess and I met up at the premises of the television station. The truth, I had low key expected a huge disappointment. Maybe we would get there and find no one, or something funny would happen. But no, primary school students were already seated in large numbers, waiting to go in for the studio recording session. Wow! *this is for real.* My face lit up in excitement.

George arrived not too long after in an army green Sienna bus. I do not know who was dirtier, the bus or its passengers. It really looked like one that had been driven through the mud. I was quickly turned off. Nevertheless, you know, even if the bus was clean, I just have always had a bias against Sienna vehicles. It's neither a bus nor a car size, in between, and always seems like the owner is trying to adopt austerity measures. Using the same car to hawk commodities around town in the day, rent it out as a pickup truck on weekends and then try to package it for church on Sunday. It reminds me of a meme circulating on Instagram recently where someone said he ordered an Uber ride and a Sienna showed up. Sienna owners have really suffered o!

They hurriedly came out of the car and moved towards us. No excessive pleasantries since contestants were already waiting. The recording studio was open so we all marched in. It was a two-part Knock out session where the final contestants were going to be determined for the grand finale at a later date. Participating schools had paid a certain amount to obtain the form. After several rounds and segments, we were left with four schools going to the finals. It was the replica of Children Shows where a studio audience would cheer on as contestants made their points in a debate or quiz competition. Was it fun for the kids? Of course. But for us, it was hardly so because not only did we not have a break, we also didn't have anything to eat.

The kids were exhausted as well, so we had to call it a day. I had put up my best performance regardless, smiling all through and ensuring the camera did not catch a glimpse of my actual tired face. Princess, on the other hand, was not having it. The director had to put her through several takes, and at a point, she almost walked off set. There was no justification for her not to. George and his shabby team did not mention anything about a costume or makeup; they just assumed we'd have it all together. Princess could stand only little of that, and she made it clear. Looking back, I would have done the same thing. No one should ever be so excited about a deal that they forget to state the

modalities in clear terms. Both parties must be on the same page.
It was about half past six. Princess and I tried to find snacks as the
vendors within the premises had closed. Even if we tried to walk
outside the premises, we would not find any drink because one of the
schools' chaperons had mentioned how far he had to walk to get gala
sausage rolls for his students.

George suddenly disappeared, and we had no idea where he'd gone. We
wondered alongside his team members, two guys who had been
running errands for him. They feigned ignorance about George's
whereabouts, but you could see through their lying eyes. George finally
showed up, and this was well past 7 pm. I was angry for having no
choice but to ride in that Sienna of his. The plan was to head to a hotel
they had booked for us in town since we couldn't travel again that day.
Also, we agreed to come back later to shoot the final round of the
completion, but first, we needed to eat.

George started to drive around as if in search of a lost pin. It took us
yelling at him to make up his mind about a restaurant to take us. Wait for
it. You would not believe that this guy stopped by a roadside food
vendor and ordered rice and beans and one meat each. *Jehovah Nissi!* The
beans were so hard it seemed like strokes of cane landing on my back as
I reluctantly chewed. It was disgusting. Honestly, if we knew that was
his plan, we would have found our way even if we barely knew the town.
But again, we were stuck with him since he was driving to the hotel
where we were supposed to spend the night. Moreover, he needed to
pay us for the day's job. None of this had been done, so we kept our
cool.

I'd never been to such a rotten hotel. We would soon land in trouble and
find out that it had no billboard or a name. By the time we arrived at the
hotel, it was almost 9 pm. When comedians make jokes about terrible
hotels, believe them. The towel looked like it hadn't been washed from
the last use. There was a yellow cube of soap that smelled like Tetmosol
inside a small green bowl. Only one tap flowed well, and the control
panel had cracked such that you needed to be very cautious while trying
to turn it open so the exposed metal doesn't cut your finger. Sigh. We
managed to settle in since it was just that one night. Little did we know it
was going to be such an eventful stay.

George sent for us, and we soon joined him and his team at the hotel bar downstairs. We were clear that we wanted nothing to drink but to be paid our remuneration for the job. We were too tired for banters, plus these guys, we had come to realise, weren't our type. I wonder how they were able to put up an educational show. I'm not casting aspersions, but their disposition to life did not depict anything worthy of emulation. These guys were on their third bottles of beer and were already talking gibberish. I was mad. We demanded our payment, and George immediately inferred that we were pretending not to understand what was happening.

What the hell is going on? He looked at the hotel attendant, and they both shared a mischievous smile. It was similar to what they did on our way into the hotel, and the attendant had mentioned something like *'oga na short time? Okay na ST abi?'* I naively thought a short time meant that we weren't staying for long. I would later understand what short time actually meant; quick sexual intercourse between a commercial sex worker/willing partner and their client[s]. We were mistaken for sex workers. It then occurred to me why the attendant looked at us in some sheepish manner. He must have thought all sorts. George managed to hand me a total of N6,500. I lost it. What *is this? Is this what you're paying us? After all the stress!* All our ranting fell on deaf ears as they were getting tipsier. We stormed away angrily and made our way to the hotel room. Hardly had we settled in bed when we started hearing strange knocks on our door. Who *is there? Hello? Who is it? There* was no response, but the knocking persisted. We concluded it must be the other room, but we were wrong. The knocking continued. We tried to find the room intercom but guys, the telephone receiver was broken. There was no directory, so even if it worked, we had no idea what number to dial. My heart was beating fast, and I began to read out crazy headlines in my head. *'Female Corps members gruesomely murdered in a hotel room in Abeokuta, the Ogun State capital;' 'Corps members raped and murdered in Ogun State;' 'Unknown gunmen kill batch B Corps members in an unknown location in Ogun State.'* Hay God!

Princess was dating a popular journalist so she called him if we needed media escalation. We mounted heavy objects behind the door and pushed forcefully against it, so they don't overpower us in case they broke down the door. We would fight back, but the heavy objects would be an obstacle while we find a way to escape. It was like a bad movie scene.

They later started calling our names, *'Titi, Princess, open this door now, wetin dey worry you?'* The voice was George's. *Wait, whaaaatt?* Apparently, they had done this with other ladies - invite them to anchor the show and warm each other's bed at night. But as they tried so hard to do the same to us to no avail, they decided to go violent. We refused to answer but pushed the bed further towards the door. We also put the chairs and every other item we could lift in the room to serve as a barricade to the door. We began banging the door as well.

As they banged, we banged back. That went on for about an hour. The silence after was deafening, and we wondered how the hotel attendants had not intervened. It became clear they were accomplices. Our eyes were open all night. Princess was in tears about how her boyfriend had warned her to run a check before going, but she trusted my judgement. I felt bad. I thought of reaching Yomi in the middle of the brouhaha, but he wouldn't show any concern. He just left us to find our way. I expected him to call George, put forward a threat that none of us must be harmed. But no, the sucker left us hanging. 6:30 am the following day, we picked our bags and raced out of the hotel; nameless, useless, no budget, short-time hotel!

I shared an abridged version of the encounter with my mom as I knew she couldn't handle the full story. My uncle, Diran Fashesin, whose family I lived with in Osogbo encouraged me to get the video of the programme so I could archive it. He didn't know that I deleted and blocked George's contact on the bus on my way back home. *Kámápàdé mọ.* [May we not meet again]. He should eat the recording.

My pastor, Tolulope Aladesami, would, a few weeks after, tag me in a post on Facebook. It was the show. It aired on TV. It was me, in my green round neck *dashiki* top and black pair of pants. She seemed very proud of me. I smiled.

We made no attempt to report. Was there any case? Yes. But it would be our word against theirs. We feared people might even blame us for being foolish, or why did we go to a hotel with the guy if we did not have ulterior motives? It is sad because there were going to be too many angles to the issue. First, we could be accused of moonlighting, which was a prohibited in the National Youth Service Corps. However, we obtained due permission from our employers.

Besides, endless accusations would have dominated the conversation, and we would end up regretting we ever spoke about it. Is that not the case with rape victims? If they speak immediately, they are judged. If they delay reportage, nothing changes. The ones who manage to go through the adjudication process hardly reached the stage of prosecution of the offender. Even if it gets close, society will wade in to guilt-trip the victim into forgiveness. We need to do better. Sigh.

Chapter Thirteen

Chronicles from the mountain top
'We must be tolerant but not ignorant'.

I totally enjoyed my National Youth Service Corps year; every bit of it. It was like I ticked off everything I wanted to do, well, except saving 90% of my allowance. I blew all of my *allowy* on clothing and maybe transportation to my Place of Primary Assignment. More so, I became editor of the editorial board that published the NYSC magazine, got my choice Place of Primary Assignment - a broadcasting firm and a much-appreciated accommodation with Uncle Diran Fashesin and family. I couldn't have asked for more.

Mother, as we fondly call Uncle Diran's wife, showed a high level of commitment to family, relationships and unshaken bravery as quiet as she seemed. The family had a structure, and I quickly blended with that. Mother made the meals, and before I attempted to help out, she was already done. It looked like magic, but she never missed one day of putting food in my lunch box. What a wonderful woman.

The State's Broadcasting Corporation had, and still has, a pull of thorough-bred professionals - Newscasters, Editors, and Analysts. I was quickly posted to the News and Current Affairs Department. Wait, that was after a short audition where Engr. Remi Omowaiye, the then Special Adviser to the Governor on Electronic Media, who is now the State's Commissioner for Works and Transport, had asked us corps members to write an article on a national topic. My submission quickly stood out, and Engr. Omowaiye picked keen interest in me on professional grounds partly because he found out we attended the same secondary school but majorly because he judged my writing brilliant.
I became a choice Corps member, if I say so myself. I also felt some

pressure not to let Uncle 'Diran down since he was known by many of the staff at the Broadcasting Corporation. He was not just known; he was respected. Uncle Diran is an excellent administrator and civil servant to whom the Governor could give important assignments and go to sleep. He delivered ever so effectively.

I worked every day, morning till evening, because I really loved the News and Current Affairs Department, especially as I was posted to a reportorial unit with Mr. Kolade Apata. Oh, great boss! He was never afraid to let us fly. It was not long before Mr. Olusola Ajiboye, the then Head of Department, began to put me on the News at 3 pm and Saturday morning Newspaper review. Typical of state broadcasting corporations, a few people raised an eyebrow about how I was too young on the job to be on air, but he turned deaf ears. He continued to take a chance on me. I'll never forget.

One of the sweet spots was when we went on outstation reportorial. It was usually fun. From the driver cracking us up with his silly jokes in his thick, funny Ijesha accent to jests about the ladies the male senior staff had been with. The drives were always points for many revelations about the organisation and the people. Call it gossip. You'd be right. It was when I began to realise that almost every leader, no matter how highly placed, has some chapters they don't read out loud, a vice, a bad habit, something, but that doesn't change the influence they wield because success seems to have a way of making up for people's flaws. Mr. Olusola Ajiboye, would appreciate my joining every important reportorial assignment because he noticed how eager I was to work; I never complained. So, I often fell into the *A list* reporting assignments, which fetched me lots of 'brown envelopes' at the time. But, please, don't judge anyone. It was simply appreciation that did not affect professional delivery in any way.

That day, the assignment was a religious event at a popular *Orí Òkè* [prayer mountain] in Ede. It wasn't my first time hearing about *orí òkè,* but this one was a constant on many radio station adverts. The inquisitive human that I am, I wanted to unravel this *orí òkè* idea. It is believed that people went there to offer prayers on knotty life issues, and there was a general belief that prayers were better answered on the mountain than in the valley. I had ignorantly imagined that it was some really high hill top where everyone had to climb to the highest point to feel closer to God. *Abi*, why will someone not pray in their home or place of worship if the mountain didn't offer some proximity to God and tourism attraction.

But again, I had heard many stories about things that happen on the mountain: how people inherited others' problems and all whatnot. We were supposed to cover one day out of the founding anniversary program of the mountain/commission. I had attended a religious event prior to that where the founder, a woman, arrived in a convoy of men in red and black overalls and golden crowns, guarded with frankincense on either sides and chants of words that neither sounded like English nor Yoruba, which I understand clearly. It was tough placing my head on what was going on, but I managed to carry out the report without stepping into the premises or eating the party pack handed me at the end of the celebration. I prayed under my breath for the most part because each one for his own belief. We must be tolerant but not ignorant.
....
All was set for Ede, and we left, Saheed Adekunle, one of the station's finest, a Yoruba reporter and I. The event was a weeklong, and we were only there to cover the ordainment of new ministers, which would take the entire day. I was excited. The ride was smooth, and all went well until we arrived at the venue, and I was denied access. Hian. *How? What happened? Why me?* I was the only female, so I began to think that maybe there was a protocol women had to follow. Their first complaint was my hair. '*Ah, she's not wearing a scarf*'.

By then, I had understood fully what was going on. My sky-blue faded jeans, and matching blue body top was a big 'red flag' on top of the conspicuous ankle boots that stood out on their own from afar. If I had known of the assignment before the day, maybe, I'd have simply worn a dress and flat, regular shoes. Or maybe not, but here we were. I did not think the rules of members needed to be binding on me since I was on a professional assignment, but you see, religion always wins in this part, so I was left to my plight. There was no going back because how would I have travelled back to Osogbo alone and then tell the boss I was frog marched from the premises because of my outfit. I knew no one would take my side. This was a religious conviction that could breed too many sentiments. So, I had to sort myself out.

Someone offered me a scarf, but I declined because I wasn't even convinced of their intentions. I was getting so worked up and angry but the church's Public Relations Officer, such a kind man, understood, so he let me into the premises but not into the main hall. That way, I could hear all that was going on, which helped me write a good report. Saheed came to join me so I would not be alone outside.

I saw all sorts of people and behaviour that made me realise that there are so many sides to this thing called life. Some people had not eaten for days or drunk anything. They were busy offering prayers and supplication. I began to wonder what could be the issue. What could they be going through? Some even lived there on the mountain for weeks, months and years, we were told. That even made me reject the wrapper brought to me to 'cover up' my bum tucked decently into my fitted blue jeans. *Who was it from? What had they used it for? Abeg.* I'll pass. We were later told that the main mountain was not what we'd seen; it was another journey further into the premises and was exclusive to few users. I hoped they found answers. I hope we all do.

Chapter Fourteen
So You want a Job
'Recruiting agencies need to do better. It is as if they think the vacancies are to be filled by animals.'

One of the things I feared most after my National Youth Service Corps was going broke. I feared it so much it dominated my mind the whole one hour, thirty minutes' trip back to Ibadan from Osogbo, where I had been serving. I lived with an amazing family friend, Uncle Diran Fashesin, who challenged me a lot about life, hard work and success with our many evening banters. He read a lot and was a choice staff at the State's Secretariat, where he worked as a director. It was an absolute pleasure staying with his family. Father, as we all called him, would spend many nights reading at his study table; one would wonder if he had an examination he was preparing for.

I once asked him how he could afford an apartment of his own in the crème de la crème area of the city and a few other things. He then began to school me about finance. It was when he let me know I might be storing shoes worth a fortune in my wardrobe and not know it. He went on to say that at the time he was building his house, he had to make a lot of sacrifices to ensure adequate funds were saved up for the project. But as at this time, I had invested heavily in my wardrobe and was so worried I'd be bankrupt the minute after passing out parade. That was exactly what happened. Good thing however is that, I had also invested a lot in myself by working so hard and so it was not an entirely hopeless situation.

The ride back to Ibadan was so smooth and fast, all I could feel was anger that the journey hadn't been long enough to afford me the luxury of time to think my post-NYSC life through. It felt like everyone was moving so fast, and I was reluctant to even get off the bus when the driver shouted, *'Iwo Road bọọlẹ'* [those going to Iwo road should come down].

....

My first attempt at job hunting was a Customer Service opening that my sister had brought to my attention through a certain church member. It seemed like a big break from just sending Curriculum Vitae to various organisations. This one was an actual job interview, and there was a written test attached. I quickly sent my CV to the church member whose firm was in charge of the recruitment exercise. In good faith, I knew I'd perform well; I mean, customer service was one of the fields I admired so much.

We were told to pay a thousand naira each to obtain the application form for the job. Hmmm, if that was now, I'd have considered that a complete red flag, but I was too naïve and maybe desperate then, to notice. How much sense does it make for applicants to be paying for forms to fill vacancies at a company that already paid the recruiting agency to do so or whatever arrangement there was just didn't make any sense to me now that I reminisce. Anyway, more than a thousand of us paid the cash and filled the form which was later submitted to the agency. According to them, the openings were for one of the country's popular mobile network providers, so all hopes were high that this was authentic.

Let me, however, not talk about how many of my highly influential, popular and brilliant schoolmates I ran into at the venue. Ah! It was a shock to see some of these people who had graduated a few years before me still in between jobs. As a matter of fact, I couldn't believe my eyes when I saw Tanito [not real name], all dressed in a colourful two-piece with a slightly bluish waist coast and 5-inch stiletto heels. I was super sure she was on the interview panel. We bantered for a bit before she spilled the beans that we were both there for the same reason. For a minute, my heart sank, and I felt pity for her. These were the brightest minds in university here hustling for a N30k job offer. Wow, just wow! We had been waiting all morning for the supposed rounds of interviews or tests to start, but no one had even come to address us or anything. It was just all rough and crappy. So many speculations and conflicting info.

It was finally test day, and I was so ill. If the job hadn't meant so much to me, I swear I'd have stayed back. I squatted half the time as I struggled to stand for long and went straight home after getting past the completely rigorous exercise. No, it wasn't a tough test; the process was what nearly ripped us all apart. Recruiting agencies need to do better. It is as if they think the vacancies are to be filled by animals because the process sometimes is simply overbearing with remuneration not commensurable with job description and expectations. I once saw an advert call for a chartered accountant with at least two years' experience. Guess the salary offered? N30,000 monthly!

We waited on results like a pregnant woman counting down to her Expected Date of Delivery. Or maybe it was just me because my incessant calls to the recruitment agency to find out the next step would tell. I always have high expectations, and I'm only learning to regulate them now because, trust me, they are freaking high, even of myself. I once expected a Nigerian bank to notify me that one of the referee accounts I had submitted for my corporate account had signatory issues. I mean, if you could send me alerts and other transaction notifications, what on earth stops you from letting me know that I wouldn't have access to the corporate account I had been remitting all my business proceeds into due to the faulty referee account? It took countless visits to the banking hall to discover. I thought these were simple customer service practices. Imagine how high my expectations were then since this was an actual customer service job. If you cannot display a great customer service experience to prospective staff, then how do you expect them to treat customers when hired? How!
Well, no calls, no emails, no feedback, nothing came. *Alaye*, our N1,000 went for nada! Multiply N1,000 by over a thousand applicants. Omoooo X 1000!

Chapter Fifteen

Good Riddance

'A conversation always gives people away no matter what they wrote on their Curriculum Vitae'.

I was working as a Personal Assistant to Mrs. A, a woman I'd describe as one of a kind. On this job, I woke up to a lineup of WhatsApp voice notes that started with 'Titi!' I'll never understand how Mrs. A's voice managed to scare and soothe me at the same time. Mrs. A is the kind of woman that dares just anything, is not bothered so much about reputation or what anyone thought of her. She always did what she had to or wanted to, regardless. I miss her voice and often intimidating yells hardly at me, but often at other staff. Deep down was a woman you'd probably never understand even if you tried. She was and is in a class of her own, really.

Anyway, I was working not just as her Personal Assistant but also managed her new business, which by the way, was the talk of the town, earning me rounds of radio interviews and endless mobile phone conversations. I want to believe I developed my phobia for ringtones working that job. Ringtones were my most dreaded sounds.

I still had my occasional side gigs as I had my weekends off. Sometimes, I'd get offers to compere at events. I had gotten one of such hosting gigs by a former classmate. He had invited me to moderate an event for his organisation, and I could not but honour it. It was him I asked to be my accountability partner when I found out about my dissatisfactory grades in our first year.

I was really willing to up my grades in the following session so I could finish well. I'm not sure he understood my concern or the level of trust it took to open up as he casually brushed off the topic and moved on to discussing other things. I don't blame him. He was probably consumed with his plans to switch faculties. He later did.

I'm glad I took the step because deep down, it pushed me, and I didn't want to fail myself or him. I had to finish well, and I did. Accountability partners, or whatever name you want to give them, are important to help us achieve our goals because, when rightly selected, they challenge us to do better, whether in the way they drive themselves to growth or the subtle criticisms they give us.

I had combined a blue pair of jeans with a yellow camisole and black jacket, crowned with my black ankle shoes, which I acquired from my sister's wardrobe not long before. It was a semi-casual occasion, so I did not need to be too dressy, but I looked the part as usual. I never take my appearance for granted because I believe it is the first impression anyone makes of you before you get the chance to speak.
This guy had come as one of the guest speakers, and I was finally putting a face to the popular name.

Everyone was trying to catch up at the end of the event when he walked up to ask for a chat. Then a chat became a talk, which ended in an exchange of digits. I could tell he fancied me, and I fancied him back. Who doesn't like a handsome, highly cerebral Mandela Washington fellow? He had pictures of him shaking hands with Barack Hussein Obama splashed all over Facebook. So, we quickly agreed to go on a date. I was newly single and was ready to make friends. The venue was one of the latest fancy malls in town, and it was supposed to be a hangout to have drinks maybe but mostly talk. I enjoy deep, intelligent, intellectually stimulating conversations tucked in between deliberate glances and coordinated stares into the other person's eyeballs. It is how you can connect with someone beyond their physical appearance or WhatsApp display picture.

The well-trained, courteous, sophisticated young lady that I was, and still am, I quickly set out thirty minutes before our agreed date time because I didn't want to keep a gentleman waiting, only if I knew the scoops of ignominy that awaited me that Sunday evening. There were no Taxify, Uber, or any of these fancy transportation companies then, and I had no car so I had to go on an okada. Gosh, all my '*baffs*, still saw me stretching my legs to climb the seat of the motor bike, while holding tightly to the iron handle behind the tilted seat so I don't fall off when the bike entered a pothole. Arriving at the venue, I looked around to see if he was already waiting somewhere since he did not have the courtesy to mention he'd be running late when I rung him earlier to let him know I was on my way. I quickly got myself busy; I can't remember with what, but it could be a book or perhaps I was simply window-shopping at the closest store in the mall. I was fuming, but I didn't call because if he was running late, he owed me a call instead. *I be high standard then sha*. Maybe the more mature me would have simply called to find out. This would have been simple courtesy and not me acting cheap. Something could have genuinely delayed him.

He strolls in at about thirty minutes past date-time, beaming with so much charm; such a cutie I couldn't resist, so I waited for an apology. *'Oh I'm sorry, it was traffic;' 'I'm really sorry I kept you waiting;' 'I apologise for delaying you, my dog died, and I had to conduct a quick funeral'*... Unfortunately, I heard nothing but endless schmoozing about his past, present, and planned accomplishments.

Oh no, I was beyond irritated. He barely let me speak. It was like a bad movie scene. It reminded me of Gabrielle Union, in *Daddy's Little Girls,* when she was trying several blind dates and landed in the hands of this afro-headed, loud and clueless guy who talked while chewing, carelessly stretching his hands over the table, making heads turn irritably as he stupidly hit his fork against his plate to make a beat for his budding rap career at 40. I was looking for an opportunity to cut in and politely bring the date to an end since he totally forgot he was not the only one at the table. *This guy hasn't learnt much from Barack Obama, has he?* Or he'd have been courteous enough to listen to me as well. A conversation always gives people away no matter what they wrote on their Curriculum Vitae. I don't think I was suffering from social anxiety but I picked my outings a lot and would only step out if it was absolutely necessary. I am not the friend you'd ring up for an unplanned occasion. I would throw you a thousand and one questions that'd have you second-guessing even your conviction to go. Maybe that's why my sister says I'm too *ko-ko-ko*. But I complain of never having anywhere to go.

I began to blame myself for stepping out. We chatted a bit more, but it was mostly about him; he barely knew anything other than what job I did.

One would have thought I'd learnt until I found myself out with him again. This time, it was in the day, and we were getting quite fond of each other by then. But I'd soon realise, all we did still was talk about him and his many ambitious aspirations He hardly cared to know me, no E for effort at all.

I would later lose his contact on purpose, and that really was good riddance to bad rubbish.

Chapter Sixteen
Palace Chronicles
Making a mistake is way better than feigning perfection.

My short stint with broadcasting remains one of the major preparatory phases of my life. I wept, learnt, and I know what that meant. All the zeal I took away from serving at the State's broadcasting corporation in Osun was all I needed to get myself integrated into my new role as a reporter and producer cum many other things the Head of Programmes Department deemed fit for me to handle. I feel like I was always ready and available for work. Now I know that could both be a blessing and a burden. The idea of striving to be liked and become a choice staff landed me into so many unpleasant circumstances I sometimes regret but mostly appreciate because had I not gone through it, I'd never have known what would be the case. You thought I would say I'd never have learnt the things I know now? No. I probably would have, anyway.

I remember doing a show, standing in for a colleague one time, and I was not surprised when I got a call from the Head of Department, blasting the living daylight out of me. It must have been worse off to know that I'd still do the show the following day. Imagine the tension and anxiety, and it was a socio-political programme, so you couldn't simply talk through as many presenters would do. You needed to have the facts right. Let's just say I was busy fact-checking in my head that I forgot I had an audience to engage. Those were my days of obsession with perfection. Thank God I now know that a perfect human, presenter or mom or friend or boss, or anything, does not exist. The unrealistic standards I had in my head kept getting in my way, and I never wanted to make any mistakes. I now do all the things I fear because making a mistake is way better than feigning perfection.

Of all the many experiences I had, good, bad, and horrid, our visit to the palace of the *Ọọni* of Ife stands out. It was a personality interview radio show, and my role was to scout for prominent personalities as guests on the show: politicians, professionals, captains of industries, and business tycoons, mostly men because there was another interview programme exclusive for women.

It was the *Ọọni* of Ife's first anniversary on the throne, so I had spoken with Mr. Ayo George, popularly known as the brain box, who I knew had a personal relationship with the monarch, His Imperial Majesty, Oba Adeyeye Eniitan Ogunwusi, Ojaja' the second. Mr. Ayo often spoke of his several engagements with the monarch, it was a no brainer that I'd ask him to link us up for an interview. Young, vibrant, good looking, and the absolute rave of the moment, *Ọọni*'s interview would be a crowd-puller for the rather conservative radio programme.

The brain box graciously offered to organise the link up for the interview, and we set out: me, the anchor of the show, with his friend, also a colleague. The arrangement was that the king was hosting an event in the palace, so we would seize the opportunity to request an interview since he hadn't granted us any appointment. However, I relied on the plan because, in my estimation, the monarch and the brain box were a phone call or text message away from each other. I thought wrong. We arrived the venue at about 4 pm since we planned a sleepover.

It was my first time, and the general reception was warm. It was a large hall with a purple rug that had a drawing of a golden emblem and then a white high chair mounted on a pulpit. Before then, I had seen pictures of that place on people's social media, who had either gone on a visit, tour or something. They'd manage to get a shot of themselves sitting below the pulpit area while the king simply stretched his sceptre across in acknowledgement of the people who paid him obeisance. The ambience was even warmer in person.

I've always loved royalty and once planned to marry a prince or someone from a royal family with prospects of becoming a crowned King, so I'd look out for surnames with '*Adé*' [Crown] or '*Oye*' [a royal position] or any clue that said they had chances of becoming the king someday. Vanity! Well, I married a king. Oluwatobi, and we are building a beautiful empire together. Hopefully, we will reign in an actual palace someday.

I was smiling broadly all through because there was just something sweet about the palace. Also, the king was hosting a cultural event where a student of Obafemi Awolowo University had won a certain contest and was being presented her gift of a brand-new Toyota. I'm not sure the brand but let's call it Toyota because it's the friendliest first car I've seen. Great second-hand value, strong parts, fuel efficient and all. I might be wrong; I am not a car dealer, I only digress. Dark skinned, beautiful, slightly tall, and absolutely warm young lady, as I guessed from afar, I couldn't help but agree she deserved the award.

She oozed a Yorubaness that reminded me of the 'Ọmọlúàbí' ethos of the Yoruba. Kneeling as she made her speech, constantly recognising the elderly ones, and her command of English and Yoruba gave her a sense of attractiveness that was clear on the faces of all in the audience. Even *Kábíèsí* was beaming with smiles and admiration of her poise. Asides from the car gift, she would have the opportunity to travel the world with the King as a culture representative and a year's supply of native attires in different styles and types. There was also a cash prize. The king couldn't see us until about 10 pm after dinner at his quarters. A few of us were moved to the dining room after the ceremony. It felt different but beautiful. The scripture about dining with kings came to my mind. Some monarchs from the Benin Kingdom had also come to pay the king homage, so we all ate together.

The interview was relaxed and enjoyable, and you would hardly tell we were speaking with one of the most influential monarchs on the continent. There are existing controversies about who the highest-ranking monarch in the Yoruba Kingdom is.

Apart from Ile-Ife being adjudged the cradle of Yoruba civilization, history has it that the reign of the Late Adesoji Tadeniawo Aderemi, who was *Ọọ̀ni* of Ife for 50 years [1930-1980] was critical to the elevation of the Ooniship being perceived as the most powerful monarchical position in the Yoruba land. Oba Adesoji Aderemi was a strong political icon who held several positions within the Regional and

Central Governments in Nigeria. Adesoji Aderemi was the Governor-General of the Western Region. He had a close relationship with the then premier of Western Region, Chief Obafemi Awolowo. A picture published by an old magazine showed the late Aderemi presenting a letter of right to the throne to Alaafin of Oyo, Oba Lamidi Adeyemi III in 1970. For many, this gesture clearly settles the controversy. However, some do not fail to bring up the conversation when it suits their interests.

Ọọni Adeyeye Eniitan Ogunwusi Ojaja II wondered why I was the only female in the team and what role I was assigned. We chuckled over banter, and he was really charming.

You could tell his keen interest in youth development and agriculture and that he is an incurable optimist. That's the idea behind his *otiseese* [It is done] mantra. He chanted that a lot in the course of our interactions, and he looked like he meant it. *Otiseese,* Nigeria would get out of underdevelopment; *otiseese* our youth will be skilled and able to effectively assume leadership positions; *otiseese,* this nation would rise again; poverty, unemployment, insecurity, kidnapping, banditry, electoral violence, and other characteristics of underdevelopment will be no more. *Otiseese.* It sounded like he was describing the kingdom of God; it was so real, so believable.

Something happened, however, that has stayed with me ever since. No one was expected to stand while speaking with the King. It was an unspoken norm, everyone simply conformed to kneeling on the rug near his throne or sitting while talking with him. Throughout the interview, all three of us were in that position. We didn't sit on a chair. We were not offered one, neither did we ask. We only followed the existing protocol. We are Nigerians and Yoruba. Just like people are asked to speak at events and they start with the popular anthem, 'permit me to stand on existing protocols'. Only that in our case, we 'sat' on existing protocols.

When next I get the chance to see the king, my fashion would be more deliberate. You would wonder why I said so. I was dressed in a short, peach, lace dress, exactly the length of my knee, with a big bow at the back, leaving the front plain and simple. There had been several warnings about how a woman must be careful when visiting a monarch in Yorubaland because if she was so attractive and the king took a liking to her, he might '*gbẹ̀sẹ̀ le'* [put his foot on her, literally acquire her as a wife by Royal fiat].

I know I said I liked royalty, but not in this way. So I thought to tone down my dressing in my mind. My colleagues had even made a joke about how I should be careful and not apply make-up. But as we knelt through the interview session, I struggled to stretch my legs because of fear that I might be a distraction since my dress was short. I had a knee ache the whole time, and I had to exchange squatting positions from left to right at intervals to relieve the *pajapaja* – pins and needles in my toes and numbness from butt to toes.

A jumpsuit, full traditional regalia or something longer would have saved the day for me - even a simple wrapper from the waist to floor. I don't own any regalia, so that leaves us with the jumpsuit option, by the way. Of course, I have a wrapper.

Another group of people were waiting to see kabíèsì as we wrapped up conversations with him. Among them was a white man. He had a clear British accent which gave him away apart from his skin colour. The king's aides had begun adjusting as if bracing up for his turn to see their boss. They were adjusting their sitting positions, looking left and right, and signaling to one another. I could guess the man wanted to pitch an idea to the king about construction. I don't have details.

But as we made to leave, the aides quickly brought a chair for the white man seeing he had refused to sit on the floor like others. He simply stood there addressing the king. He also didn't bow as others. I watched in amazement. W*hat does this mean?* I felt pity for myself after kneeling for half an hour in my short dress! We dared not have asked for a chair! We revered tradition over our comfort.

The floor wasn't bare. There was a thick, fluffy rug. It was inviting, but the man stood. If anyone needed to sit on a chair, it would be us because handling the microphone and adjusting sitting positions simultaneously was not such a convenient task if we needed to get a great sound. Yet, here was someone else simply doing what's convenient for him regardless of what had been the norm. Again, I am reminded about how some norms are only social constructs, not immune to modification.

I looked at the king's reaction; he didn't bother. Nothing seemed off. Everyone moved on, but I could not. It got me thinking how we never question behaviour, and we just follow the norm. Maybe we could have asked for a seat instead of struggling to balance the microphone between the distance from the floor to the Ọọ̀ni's throne. I posted the experience and pictures on Facebook. Of course, various opinions followed in the comment section, and someone even rudely asked if Christian Amanpour would have sat on the floor to interview the monarch. He was implying that we lacked professionalism and courage. I wonder if he would have acted differently. It's easier to criticise a thing you're not part of. We were paying respect to the cultural belief systems whether it was convenient for us or not. Apparently, culture can be revised; it would only take one person looking from another direction.

I suspect *kabíẹsi* would have obliged that we should be given a chair. He is human, and he was totally warm towards us. But then, he is always surrounded by fierce traditionalists-sticklers for traditional rites and norms difficult to drag into modern times.

Chapter Seventeen
The People's Department
Self-doubt is not worth it at all.

One gift I possess is the gift of perspective. The fact that I hardly assume the general view of things has helped me overcome a lot of challenges that I have encountered and still encounter in life. Also, letting go of a perfectionist, idealistic worldview has changed my life for good. To develop a healthy self-image, we must let go of the idea that we, or life has to be perfect. Everything that happens to me has taught me how to be there for me and always look on the bright side because nothing is ever perfect.

I hesitate to offer advice to people because it appears as a dangerous task. I believe that everyone needs to discover themselves and understand what works for them each time. If advice is to be offered, both parties must understand that life is not a one-size-fits-all phenomenon so what works for one person may not necessarily yield similar results for another person.

However, in the process of self-discovery, we all need support. Read books on areas where you feel deficient, connect with like minds and those already ahead of you and always believe in yourself. Self-doubt is not worth it at all.

Nevertheless, I have enjoyed support from amazing humans that a former dear friend would call *The People's Department*. I am always grateful for their timely interventions in my life's trajectory.

My parents-in-law, Mr. & Mrs. Olujimi Kusimo, who called me every day to ensure I was doing fine when I had my baby during a pandemic and felt so lonely and lost. My mom's uncle, Bamidele Akinsiku, who has extended his affection for my mom towards us her kids. My aunt, Omolara Akinsete and my mom's aunt, Mrs. Kike Bammeke, you both have constantly been in our corner, steadily showing us that we are not alone. Dr. Dayo Oyeola, thank you for your warm reception of my siblings and I. Dr. Tosin Atewologun, you're always my father. My dear Uncle Olawale Olaajiki, thank you for being there always. Pastors Femi &Tolu Aladesanmi and Rev. Niyi and Bisi Ladokun, thank you for not only preaching, but also nurturing. Alhaja Tinu Barde, one time, Sanmi and I needed to dish dinner but the light in the kitchen was off and we were both too scared to go in the dark. You suspended your conversation with our grandmother and made your way to the kitchen to switch the light on. That was so kind. Pastor Chuks Ngeronye, I just want you to know that I'm no more a tomboy although I still have my shoe racks full of boots. Professor Omolade Obateru Oladele, I'll never forget the critical role you played in kicking off my Undergraduate academic journey. Dr. Joel, you would want me to be a lawyer but I'm grateful for all your support. Pastors Kayode and Bunmi Babatunde, you love our family so much you have gone out of your way many times and I see it. God will honor you. Dear Mr. Seye Oyeleye, thank you for constantly believing in me and allowing me to fly in my professional endeavour. Mr. Jola Oyeneye, I indeed appreciate all your wise counsel and admire how you keep redefining the concept of Public Service by giving your best to your work. Aunty Ronke Giwa-Onafuwa, thank you for your mentorship and for giving a strong recommendation for my first graduate job. To my DAWN Commission family and everyone who has, and continues to show kindness towards me and humanity, you all are members of The People's Department.

Glossary

ogbanje - Its literal meaning in the Igbo language is "children who come and go". Sometimes the word ọgbanje has been used as a synonym for a rude or stubborn child.

ẹba- is a staple food mainly eaten in the West African sub-region, particularly in Nigeria and parts of Ghana. It is specifically called *Eba* by the Yoruba.

eewọ- taboo

mẹkẹmẹkẹ-The act of not being tough enough

owambe - social events held on weekends, such as weddings.

ọmọ- An exclamation or expression of surprise

wahala-unnecessary trouble

abeg-colloquial expression for the word, 'please'.

litty-litty- When something is exceptionally great, intense, and fun, as a party.

nawa- An exclamation or expression of surprise

abaya- a long piece of clothing that reaches to the ground, covering the whole body except the head, feet and hands.

amala- is a local indigenous Nigerian swallow food, native to the Yoruba ethnic group in the South western states of the country.

gbẹgịrị- is a type of Nigerian soup popularly eaten by the Yoruba tribe of Nigeria. It is made from peeled cooked bean

Ehn –an exclamation showing surprise

oyìnbo- In Nigeria, it is generally used to refer to a person of European descent or people perceived to not be culturally African.

unfoursquarian – not possessing the characteristics of the Foursquare Church

ahn ahn- an exclamation showing surprise

baffs-fashionable clothing

ko-ko-ko- describing a person who appears to serious-minded and hardly jokes

gìrìgìrì- forceful or with a sense of urgency.

aṣọ ẹbị- is a uniform dress that is traditionally worn in Nigeria and other African cultures as an indicator of cooperation and solidarity during ceremonies and festive periods.

abamieda-Used to describe the late Fela Anikulapo-Kuti

oporrr- a slang commonly used by Nigerian millenials and Gen Z to express admiration for something or someone.

danfo - A privately-owned minibus or van hired to carry passengers.

Hian- expressing displeasure over something

lmao-laughing my ass out

olekú- a popular native outfit, commonly worn by Yoruba people of Southwest Nigeria, which was a trend in the 60's

alaye- young man/ woman

allowy- monthly allowance paid by the Federal government to Nation Youth Service corps members

Look at Uche's face- a local idiomatic expression denoting the art of giving a damn or not giving a damn about a person or something.